Passions,
Dreams,
and Pain

DAVID REVELL II

ISBN: (Paperback)   979-8-9997305-0-3
        (E-book)   979-8-9997305-1-0

Library of Congress Control Number: 2025916630

Published By:

East Orange, NJ 07017
http://www.davidrevellbooks.com

Publisher Provider:

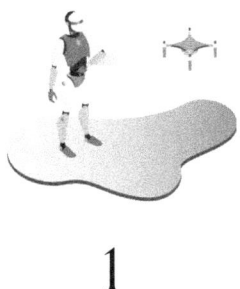

1

Facial recognition bots were spreader all over the stage at the AYZ Corporation facility. Reverend Trumbull had given the crowd a breath-taken flight to technology.

"Hold the small device towards your face, he said to the captive audience, these four foot robots are a conversation piece."

Spawning the components of the facial recognition bots, Reverend Trumbull erected a spotlight to fire up the audience.

"This monstrous light is something new that you can install outside your home," he continued, opening its innovative eye to anything that is abruptly under the functions of a username."

Ready to perform that Thursday night Avery Banks aka True Blue Imbecile followed the routine he usually did.

Asking for everything to create a laugh because laughter to him was a buried bridge to comedy.

"C'mon let's set up the scenario," he said to manager Rod English, "it's hype with the unions."

Those words from the True Blue Imbecile were a platform stranger than his air freshener. A pitch to his reckless world.

"Being one of the worst comedians out there, you need to find a way to improve their spirits," Rod said, "having his pound of flesh."

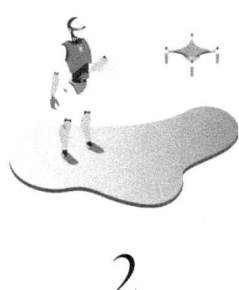

2

Sister Abner gave remarks about the presence of robots being in the church.

"It is nothing but deviltry, "she said to Lorna Loe, baking her large lemon meringue pies from a special oven courtesy of Warehouse Number One.

Her culinary business was a service that maintained a party movement. Dependent on no one.

"The problems are the building fund with the wrong people, "she continued, buried with untruths. They disrupt the whole system."

Numerous times a disagreement between her and Reverend Trumbull was now linked to the Go-ahead Employment Agency.

"Those crazy AYZ kits oh gosh, prayer is the only way we can survive," she exclaimed.

Executing her methodology as the big persona.

A lemon meringue from her airs began with a survey done by Celeste Banks. The content was enough to talk about.

"Reader's love reading about my new baking ideas," she boastfully said, "most cooks become a rising scare."

Sold on the delicious taste of lemon meringue pie Lorna rested on her promise to greet one and all to her arrangement for the Boom-Boom Room.

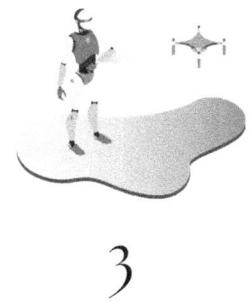

3

Confident Dr. Rainey displayed the Sunday Veil trade bot showing potential vendors photographed by freelance photographer Gertrude Hammond involved in the Hawk Foundation.

"Make it fast Miss Hammond," he said, "the future relies on it."

Trade was constantly on his mind.

"Potentially my bots are the pathways to the doors that will bring fire in the funnels. He continued, looking at the four foot robot.

Gertrude's camera began to breathe with the flash of the robot's chest screen. A number of patrons were curious about the upcoming showrooms at the Robot Campus.

"The Goppik Page makes us aware that vendors are seated at the roundtable meeting in that very building," one vendor said.

Surrounding the displayed Sunday Veil trade bot, the patrons looked at its odd-shaped device it was holding.

The face of the robot was an incredible make up of metallic blue humanoid face.

"I saw that on the Goppik Page," another patron remarked, a lot of showroom blunders"

Overhearing this and hating the moment Dr. Rainey became difficult and irate.

"Get out of here you novices!," he shouted, "that infernal Goppik Page should be done away with."

Standing by his convictions he decided to use his remote to entrap the patrons by locking the enormous doors.

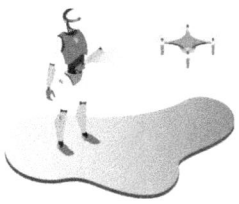

4

Revealing her identity as Brown Summer Storm to Dr. Rainey turned his head and sprung him into a new phase of life.

"That gal gives me a high and what a disguise she wears," he said to technician Larry Norton, knowing that sweetened the deal with her.

Puzzled, Larry asks "What are you talking about?"

"Don't you know Lorna Loe and Brown Summer Storm are one and the same, Dr. Rainey remarked, "she can shake that thing."

"You are a little old for her," Larry said, "she could be a gold digger."

A slight rage entered Dr. Rainey's nervous system.

"Ass!, he exclaimed, signing her up for that sex gun of hers is all I want."

Noting that her enormous breasts are greatly monitored by the Boom-Boom Room.

"V.I.P guests love to photograph her," Dr. Rainey continued, highlights are recognized as a sister holstered."

The association of Dr. Rainey and Lorna Loe was a platform that he wanted to improve upon.

"The odds are you are taking a gamble, Larry said, you are sitting on a throne with dynamite."

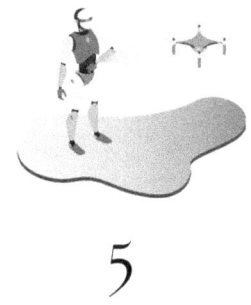

5

Testing her toy robots at the Robot Campus brought on all kinds of visions. A thought of a game's cape came when she met Quincy Ronald, a video game developer.

"Are you free to chat for a few minutes my sister? "he asked, prompting words of politeness.

The atmosphere caused Abby to remain brightened by Quincy's approach.

"Excuse me, she said.

"Quincy, he boldly said, I see you with your toys and they look armed.

The Robot Campus daily catered to newcomers especially entrepreneurs seeking to move up in the world.

"We should connect," Quincy continued, "a contender in a male oriented business can take advantage of the Goppik Page with a thrilling message."

That Thursday information about the 56th expo was also discussed wondering if Abby was the best pick for what he had in mind.

"This is a unique opportunity for you and me," he said pulling out his business card, "live chats will give you more about me."

College students loved the video games that Quincy displayed in the recreation area.

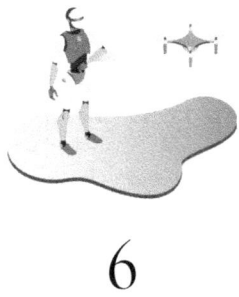

6

Many approaches to Eternal Robotics had Celeste Banks posting the robotic industry and the relations to preservation. The warehouses were visual to Dr. Rainey focusing on vendors.

"I understand there is going to be a job fair here next week," she asked the security guard, artificial intelligence through Eternal Robotics is going to be videotaped.

Failing to act on this opportunity is something to prepare for.

"A onetime fee that connects with Eternal Robotics for five learned sessions to chat about," she said, to the security guard, a marketing campaign is what I am about"

The perspective of Lorna Loe stood the month's service of Eternal Robotics representing her sex guns.

"Baby where is the connection of the internet on this" ,she said to Dr. Rainey, surfing on the screen.

The emails were addressed to Dr. Rainey often along with the Goppik page. Weighing in on the news of the day in the midst of scary events.

"Patience my dear Eternal Robotics delivers the key to the visual," he said to Lorna.

Due to the Sunday Veil trade bot which lit up the service of Eternal Robotics changed the attention of testimonials.

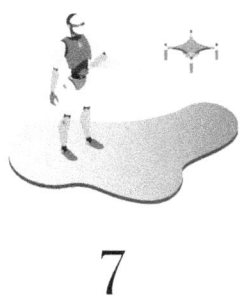

7

Wanting toys to be demonstrated Abby always criticized the ongoing campaign of Eternal Robotics.

"The challenge is the urban pathway to relationships, she said to Celeste in her tiny apartment, when prospects buy into this AYZ kits nonsense."

The morning air influenced the tradition of conversation.

"That kit I bought from W&A electronics just doesn't work, Abby continued, a waste of technology."

Unaware of a little drone circling her apartment Abby vowed to publicly expose Eternal Robotics to fraud.

"Is that what happened with the kit?" asked Celeste, "get your money back."

A fascination of Galaxy Baptist Church was the turbo two wheelers of Kara Lewis, owner of K&L Bike Shop. A few seconds of programming these robo-bikes became an experience for the church's showroom.

"Let me photograph this," Gertrude Hammond, freelance photographer said to Reverend Trumbull, "this atmosphere is exciting."

A major concern was the path to establish robotics in the church.

"Popularity of these bikes my sister has is enormous," he replied, "it is posted on several websites through K & L.com."

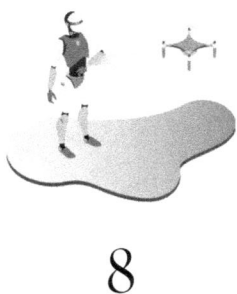

8

Young Khelic Lewis Completely intense about his partnership with the True Blue Imbecile. He had endless thoughts about how he could improve the act.

"There are possibilities that I don't have to use cheap theatrics in the act he said to his mother Kara, Avery's Giant house sneaker routine should be changed."

"You should express your opinion son," Kara remarked, "timing is everything in life."

The draw among comedians at the Boom-Boom Room inspired him to talk about it more.

"Throwing confetti disguised as potatoes at the audience is what I have in mind," he continued, "more broadcasts and podcasts about our act will do."

The imaginable recipe for comedy greatly challenged Khelic, smiling at the idea of having a gig at the Robot Campus.

"I bet we can hold the audience captive," trying to convince his mom, during the tours of the Robot Campus we can be a sideshow while the people pass by."

"I think you need to further your education first," Kara said, as a choice of wisdom.

It now proposed a problem for the young man as he confided in his mother.

"I know it is a big competitive edge"

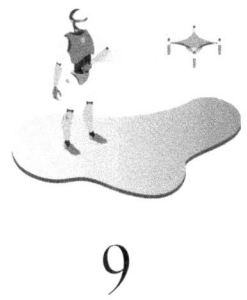

9

Editor Odessa Paulson of Gains Publications had a chance to weigh in on her widget investments. It predicted growth that would maintain a stable path to gains.

"Bo-hog!," she exclaimed, "you are directing these displays of widgets?

"Ah ain't got no hold on et," he said, da evens wood happen as ah thought."

A small package posed a thought to Bo-hog's mind.

"Ah somethin came in ya office a few minutes ago, he said, et wuz lef on ya desk"

"I didn't order anything"

"Et label says automate ya bizness,Bo-hog said, et frum Quintee Ronal."

"It's from my brother Quincy," Odessa remarked, he's talking about "growth in technology."

Deciding on opening the package Odessa chose to control her enthusiasm.

"This influences the effort to navigate guns and ammo," she continued.

"Wha gasped Bohog, wat en da package?"

Graphs were found in the box Quincy Ronald had sent plus blueprints for widget games.

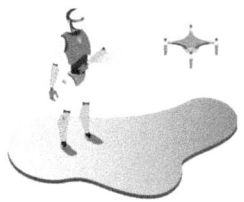

10

A video recording of daughter Odessa Paulson consumed most of her demonstrations in Apple Park. It was the 400 Robot program. A moment of technology added Park Rangers to her prospect list.

"Apple Park has reviewed the bike races demonstrating artificial intelligence," she said to one of the Park Rangers.

It is necessary for the talks about the 400 Robot program to be live to an audience.

"Thank you for your cooperation," Odella continued, with the Park Ranger.

The conversation in front of Editor Odessa Paulson was disturbing when her daughter appeared to be confused.

"Odella!," she exclaimed, there is no guarantee with your business."

Her dream was treaded on and she was furious.

"Ma I don't appreciate this," Odella said, "we have mentors to take care of doubts."

Belting out those words was another way to discourage her blueprints.

"You are not making any profits," Odessa said, you need to further your education."

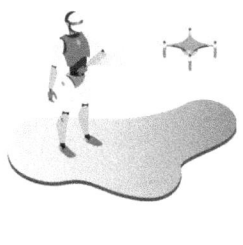

11

Credibility was always questionable when dealing with video game developer Quincy Ronald. Wholeheartedly he was determined to detail the objectives concerning a crowd of people. Standing by Detective Teague picking up one of his brochures concerning a gold miniature island.

"The Goppik Page mentions your gold opportunities in front of a computer is a must," he said to Detective Teague while in his office, All the details are through your meetings."

The left corner of Detective Teague's computer screen caused him to focus on how the miniature islands were distributed.

"Hey man!," he exclaimed, "financially I have another recipe for this"

Knowing that Quincy had a record Detective Stan Teague became suspicious of his words.

"I'm touched by your idea," Detective Teague said, vendors are upcoming and give the factors of live chats."

Viable words was an effort that Quincy tried to convey to the Detective.

"My interaction along with your gold-breathed success," Quincy remarked.

"C'mon Quincy, this is not worth my time.

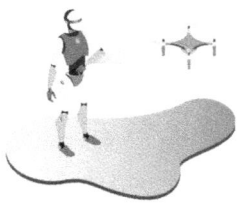

12

Wondering if the immigrants were addressed at the meeting place in her absence exercised the events of the Robot Campus. Ursa Abajoe, an immigrant officer, was seated in the conference room of Gain Publications.

"Talks don't ensure things mon, "she said to a staff member, "eerie screams from the migrants need to be dealt with."

The sky began to rumble starting with the kissing of rain wetting the awnings of the Station A upholstery store.

"We got to understand each other mon, she continued, it is a matter of chat boxes."

Her position on immigrants maintained an outlet for cameras to spy on.

"The strong and the weak are certain to range from Black and Brown through the practice of control," a staff member said, "expect the planet to have the elements of universal law."

Ursa's mind became a weight that Tuesday morning influenced with tales of Editor Odessa Paulson's widgets.

"What's holding up the editor?" "she asked the staff member; she's talking about a tried-and-true formula for the community mon."

A monitor in the conference suddenly came on and made a visual a form resembling Odessa Paulson.

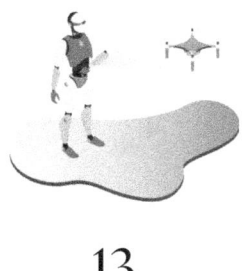

13

Wearing the same red dress Abby painted it as a replica for a female robot.

"You'll reach the top with that girl," said Celeste, the goppik page should have this"

Apple Park came to mind to show the networkers.

Upon reaching the park she was approached by Reverend Trumbull. A facial recognition device was suggested by him. This was a challenge for her.

"What do you mean?," she asked.

"Sister, I know you there's always room for improvement," Reverend Trumbull said, it is a cultural breakthrough.

AYZ kits concerning facial recognition were being handed out as samples by some of the church members already in the park.

"Together we can make big bucks, Reverend Trumbull boastfully said.

Abby showed resistance towards him.

"I have enough mentors who strengthens me," she exclaimed, so many people try to reach out to me."

14

A chance to impress Dr. Rainey with a survey on robotic faces that breathed profits was followed by a lobby show.

"Oh, it's filled with glass displays of the Sunday Veil trade bot," she said, to the security guard."

"Eternal Robotics surpasses the novelty shops, she continued with the security guard."

The Wednesday morning high rose to a great honor fresh with trades. Taking it in a positive Celeste turned to the morning air and showed a physical laser from an android phone.

"I love that Miss, Dr. Rainey exclaimed walking inside the lobby, your name?"

"celeste Banks"

The fruit of his labor she wanted to discuss.

"Oh you're that survey woman, "he said, "I'm Dr. Rainey.

Celeste's face lit up which made the curriculum exciting.

"Are you doing a survey on fail systems" he said abruptly, is this your interest?"

15

Boldly walking away Deacon Franklin bearded the atmosphere of the university campus. However, he remained vibrant. It was Apple bend City he wanted to glorify. Capturing the tourists was a thrilling challenge. The sound of the 56th expo was a contender for a job campaign. The words of the Goppik Page were not clear to him. Walking alone Deacon Franklin met Gertrude who seemed to be alive with the physical presence of an electronic bible.

"This is fascinating, Eugene it is African American art," she said, awakened mentally by her surprise, becoming a freedom fighter."

Under this impression Deacon Franklin asked a question.

"What are you saying?, he asked.

Furthering the conversation he felt she was unstable.

"C'mon C'mon it is a marvelous light," she said.

Deacon Franklin remained steadfast.

"It has the promise of support, "Gertrude exclaimed, "you can charge this bible up."

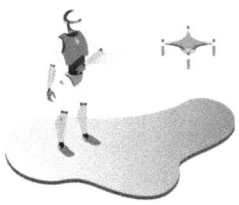

16

The agenda for Tuesday morning with breakfast was with his fiancé Kara Lewis.

Voicing his opinion on bike promotions which Kara did not base on entrepreneurship.

Limiting his attachments to the Station A mania.

Publicity that unveiled Kara's robo-bikes ramped up to moments of structure and system.

The internet explained the agenda for robo-bikes as a part of Station A upholstery store's new product. Patrons' attention to Kara's perspective is enough to start a conversation between Deacon Jansen and Kara Lewis.

"Chat box perhaps regarding the right bike at the 56th expo over the gray setting there," she said.

"Dat ah ez ah point of view.," Deacon Jansen remarked.

The fascination talks virtually connecting a visual screen in his Station A upholstery store.

"A matter of concern is your sofa that is part of Station A" said Kara.

The discussion made Deacon Jansen connect to her products.

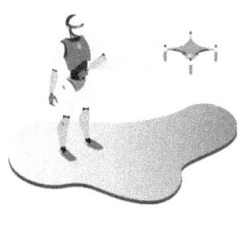

17

The atmosphere of the Boom-Boom Room smelled like beer and it maintained the night with its glowing lights.

"Avery, this thing is a brilliant thing to have Khelic say, we should launch it."

The device was from Station A.

Most of the technology was a scenario for a video monitor for Avery's gigantic house sneaker featured at the show.

"The true blue imbecile loves to aid the knee jerk reactions imposed on the audience, Avery said.

The vendors in the lobby of the Boom-Boom Room changed the potential interest of the photographs enough to talk about.

"Which way should I arrange the display? "Asked one vendor

Noting the moment was enough to be physical.

Organizing a network of comedians became intense.

"This method is kind of dated," Khelic remarked. Revell

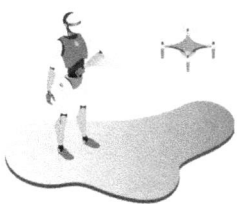

18

The light of amazement had editor Odessa Paulson addressed the links that had headlines about her widgets that cryptos appeared, I'm developing my brand Bo-hog, she said, to Sergeant Fierce, it is part of Tuesday's podcast."

Investors with intent to network for the functions of a widget bot. They had a 14-day trial on its functions.

"I know that it is a curiosity by many trades, "Editor Odessa said, looking at the professional people.

The window in her office became a view that concerned the trades under the Gains Publications was followed by R&B music.

"Hear that that's mellow," she said to the guests.

The glass displays in the conference room occupied their minds.

The color of the widget bot with the condition of a membership.

"You must converse with international trade," she said, in front of an overview."

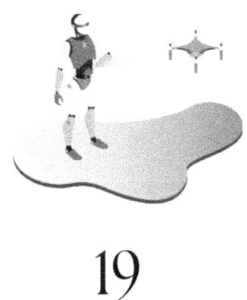

19

"A great deal of money is in the height of Apple bend City, "Odella said, stirring up the fold.

The business impression secured its heavy and large trades and uncertainty of the 400-robot program.

"It's backed by the 56th expo."

The condition of a robot sector is unique for a proposal.

"It's a hype with unions. It makes a conversation piece she continued talking to Khelic.

Methodology was the whole system for the 400 Robot program.

"Yo it's a lot of blunders," he said.

Consistency in her mind was the future of the four foot and odd -shaped devices.

"Metallic blue faces gives me a jolt to my nervous system," Odella said, "recognized as an association of all kinds of visions."

Wanting to move up in the world Odella displayed her bots in the recreation area of the Robot Campus.

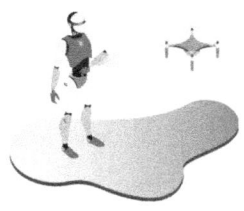

20

A game sector Quincy Ronald was developing a unique business plan.

"This is grease on Bend Street, "he said to the invited Abby Yolanda.

His apartment was everything that inspired the consumption of video games.

"I'm becoming familiar with your style," she said so positively.

Feeling he struck gold allowing the meeting to be less formal.

"I'm attuned for your salute to dinosaurs"', Abby said, who was in line with its beginnings."

Practically everything in Quincy's apartment featured goods based on activities at Apple Park.

"Oh, you have so much clutter, "she said, "are they fully funded for trade?"

A little irritated he answered, sure they are"

Certain to add profits was in the mall.

"The conditions in the city still are in the park, Abby continued.

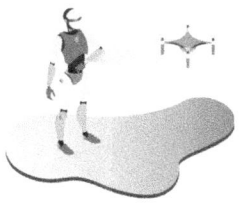

21

Contending with his miniature gold island opportunity registered with the Robot Campus vital for the background prepared for possibilities of trade. Guidelines followed on the installed monitors. The purpose of the Robot Campus is to evaluate businesses and promotions.

Detective Stan Teague exclaimed, "Its transport loaded for transport."

Designed apps became a wonderful marvel for his gold miniature islands.

"My expression of goods to reflect on means of a plan," he said to L.N. owner of the Robot Campus empire.

Business occupants of the program had a higher criterion double digits for the first time.

"Under your umbrella you handle all purposes," Detective Teague remarked.

The subject of gold armor came up.

"Visualize it man size plated armor of gold as an investor"

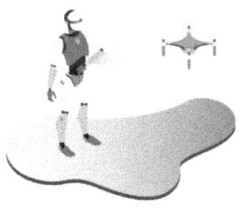

22

Ursa Abajoe's pitch to a reckless association hyped with unions. a buried scenario for usernames. Outside those offices were immigrants. These migrants were becoming a scare as the big persona that cannot survive on the streets. It was becoming a problem for the Go Ahead Employment Agency.

"They are disrupting my whole system," Deacon Franklin said, "Those people are wrong to come here."

Difficult and irate Ursa Abajoe immigrant officer relied on the Hawk Foundation.

"We need to improve upon its mon," she exclaimed, not recognized as a holstered servant.

Deacon Franklin's nervous system was shaken by her frankness.

This is a challenge of life dear heart, he said, "the migrants are not innocent."

Uncomfortable with the conversations of guns inside his electronic store Wyatt Anderson took the liberty to round off his discussion.

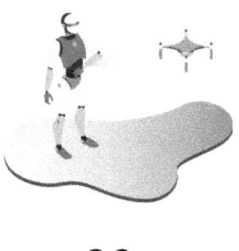

23

"The objective of the program is to proceed with the perspective of customer service," he said to Celeste Banks. Enjoying the agenda for the first time she was a natural for the W&A electronic store.

"I'm not comfortable with the competition," he continued with Celeste.

Industry giants stayed armed with comments about guns.

"A general concern brings vendors together," Celeste said hoping to get more out of him.

Bothered by more questions Wyatt decided to act on the things discussed in the industry like postcards.

"Right off the streets they have these expos, "he said.

Sustaining his belief about street vendors and the conditions of Bend Street was similar to that of Warehouse Number One.

"The photography of guns is refreshed with certainty," she said, visible to the gun gallery.

Expressing company research Celeste told him what the country needed.

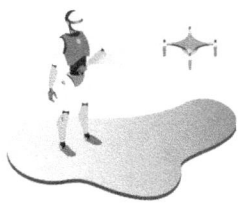

24

Pestering the street vendors Bunch Anderson caused a tantrum among them.

Doubling teaming, two opposing vendors failed to subdue the hulky 6'3' Bunch.

Faster than a blink he maintained a few powerful punches to an approaching vendor on his left. in front of another reluctant vendor blinded by his massive blow.

Nearby Detective Teague witnessed this disturbance and pushed Bunch to the side of a warehouse wall.

"Wha! the hell are you doing Teague?, he screamed with more violent outbursts, it became a problem for Detective Teague. The blinded vendor lied in a comatose state.

"You don't need to go downtown Anderson!," Shouted the Detective.

Outraged, the other vendors counted on an ambulance arriving on the scene after a 911 call.

"Arrest that mother fu***er, "one vendor shouted to sum up the situation.

The shocker drew the attention of the Gain Publication reporters.

"Each of you vendors pose as confident newsmen unique for an organization."

25

The benefits of credit lines had Congressman Anthony Darrell under a 40% utilization.

No more than 4 banks secured his currencies for his gains of digital dollars. Zero interest is what he was seeking. No upfront fees were copied by his staff.

Putting down 50% of his gold earnings to finalize the decision he had with Detective Teague.

"I have at least three accounts that has been directed to lenders'" he said to a staff member it helped them to access the most current."

Improvements from the original deal achieved so far had proven to be less effective.

"Every day I take a second glance at that miniature gold island," he continued, "with audiobooks it is explained a little better."

Postcards of Detective Teague's opportunity aimed to address his organization regarding the agreement in which were linked to EIN numbers.

"Credit scores enables one to qualify for revenue lending," a staff member said, "it opens up more levels."

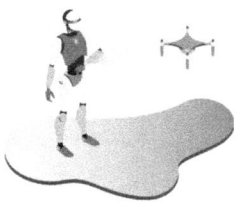

26

Choosing the trade of robotic widgets Sargeant Fierce had linked the widgets to the infamous Robot Campus. Furious he disturbed owner L.N. in front of the roundtable members of the Robot Campus meeting room.

"Ah conneck ya all witah visual screen that automat da pretinses of falsehood, he said directly to the investors'.

The quick evaluation prompted the morning with frustrations that was unpleasant for both Sargeant Fierce and L.N.

"Your insolent fool," shouted, I alone control the broadcasts."

Speaking his mind that day Sargeant Fierce provided a solution to the problem.

"Ah calm down ya goldbricks take ah look inta ya account dey kin be corrected, he said, tallee et up dem plans ain't feasible."

To maintain fairness and integrity L.N. acknowledged a few facts.

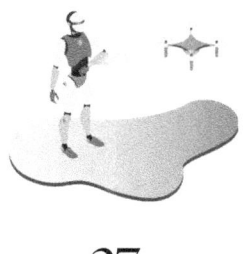

27

Fulfilling the month with orders of Sentinel Robots supervisor Tim helped to access the levels of service achieved so far as audio books.

"The drop shipment of bots is a further improvement, he said, in which further information was with the highest form of generosity."

Communicators from various companies always stressed the interest of new technology.

"Honesty at least comes from a Better Business report"Tim said to a worker, who was greatly challenged.

Smiling at the presence of the four-foot Sentinel robot he spooked the other employees by physically entering the work stations.

"Look at that face!" , one man exclaimed, "it's trying to open its mouth."

A speech came out of the Sentinel's mouth.

I am holding workers captive focus on your work the robot said

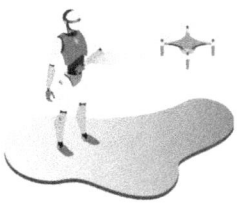

28

The half glass of wine was in front of Dr. Rainey as Larry Norton chatted about money streams of income suitable for conversation.

"You are heading for a mini-stroke attack, he said, I have warned you the last time you had one."

Weighing the glass of wine in his hand Dr. Rainey said, I'm a little more stable since I brought the novices to learn about testimonials."

Words of criticism came from Larry.

"I think that's a cry for help, he remarked, for what it is worth a sure fire way is to have live chats and at the utmost sober."

Digesting his wine and burping Dr. Rainey embedded a cherry in his glass and began to pour himself another glass of wine from the bottle.

"Bah!, he said if you want to remain in my employ you better stop lecturing me," he continued, after seizing the bottle from Larry's hand.

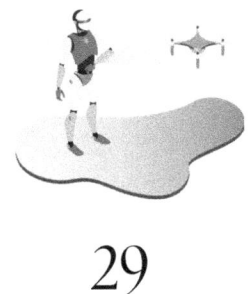

29

African American art was evaluated by Art Tutors Inc. owner Nathan Oswald using a clear picture app regarding Black history. He had many roles in mind.

Healthy minds getting through the banning of books, a breakdown of a troubled society.

"Swelling thoughts will eventually lead to a gain of higher goals'" he said to Republican Congresswoman Kathleen Wrigley, at least once a year Apple bend City should have a history seminar."

This led to better readings of history.

"Use the instructions on the Goppik page," Congresswoman Wrigley said, but it will expire in 24 hours."

College students 18 and over were pictured to be full of questions and absorbent to labels for one another.

"Eh?," Nathan reacted.

Calls and texts we get from time to time "Congresswoman Wrigley continued, "it is necessary for them to display their concerns on the internet screens."

Results were based on the relationship between student and teacher.

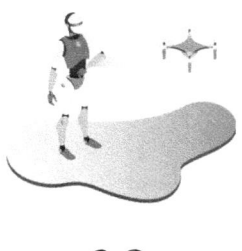

30

Hardrock gang leader of the Derelicts released to the streets a drug proven to be a sizable product for smoking and drinking. Assisting in its distribution he encouraged pick-ups from the back of the Core art center.

"Yo join the crowd schedule a talk with Bunch it will be worth yas whiles," Hardrock said to a cronie, da performin art is a great place to start."

The Core Art Center was a perfect front for HardRock and for suppliers.

"The fu**ing art events showing African American art insisting on large monitors to open an enormous curtain prompting a light created for the center of attraction."

Gently pointing to his right finger, he pressed down on a small contraption the size of a match box. It seemed to penetrate his finger with its green liquidity substance.

"This is all you need to make it through da f**ing day," he continued.

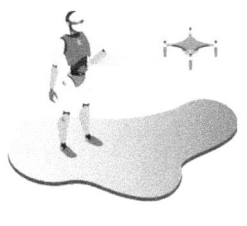

31

Chairs depicted the major staffers as suppliers to blend African American Art.

Perfect for the store he had in mind.

"The vents drew an audience position for African American art, Nathan said To Congresswoman Wrigley.

Custom storefronts were prominent for sales. The high contrast of art hooked the guest panel joining his art event.

"The purpose of this is to include everything toward grants, "he said, to Congresswoman Wrigley.

The revenue excited the Congresswoman greatly confident about it all. Introductory offers on African Art secured the month with refunds starting with thousands of cigarette paintings.

"It has its flaws, "said Congresswoman Wrigley showing a list of retail locations.

The platform online helped Nathan. Customer service for the Art Tutors displayed guides for the novice.

32

Reverend Trumbull decided to enter onstage a large visual screen connected to the stage auditorium of the AYZ corporation meeting place.

"Meet the section of the roundtable members, he said to the audience, focus on the screen, they are carrying out the business of face recognition."

Feeling that favorites began with an online. Reverend Trumbull mentioned broadcasts for beginners.

At the end of the night meeting, he left out reputation.

"Don't rely on the Goppik Page it can drive people away he continued, "we are offering free training."

An announcement of a 5 day review was in tutorial form.

Implementing the AYZ Corporation in the robotic game to build an online brand. Each day they covered a topic setting up solutions.

"We are going to give away free gifts, "he said to the audience.

33

Past the True-Blue Imbecile was love for technology routinely intense a giant sneaker prop house. Teasing the audience with his invite to tour His sneaker house inside surprises the True-Blue Imbecile by choosing a patron from the audience.

Upon walking onstage and entering the giant sneaker house the patron witnessed a crazy method of the True-Blue Imbecile. A crazy method of name calling.

"What's this?," asked The True-Blue Imbecile? walking behind the patron.

A copy on the little table was a book entitled "Looking for Comedians."

This key added another twist to the act.

"What do you see?" he continued to ask

It made quite a moment for the patron.

"It's clear to me that you are mentally disturbed, he said jokingly.

"You can get the hell out of my house," True Imbecile shouted.

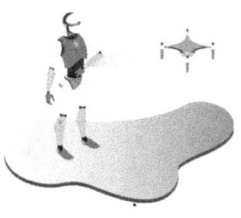

34

Changes Sister Abner wanted for Galaxy Baptist Church.

The concept of technology was not to her liking.

"The truth is the good Reverend is becoming a slut to the devil, she said to Lorna Loe.

"Change is what the church needs, Lorna said, rights and wrongs you got to recognize.

This was not clear to the elderly Sister Abner.

"Child', I have been righting the wrongs and the rights before you were born, Sister Abner said reacting to the comment.

A webinar session was featured online on behalf of Galaxy Baptist Church.

"You should watch this mama sis"

"Forget about that trash," Sister Abner insisted.

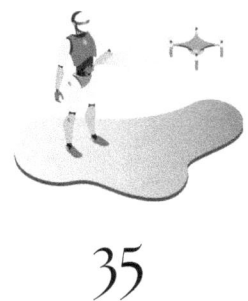

35

A mini-heart attack that Dr. Rainey had done not faze him.

Streams of income continued to challenge his mind.

"Larry, I'm going to my idea of a network to the Robot Campus, he said to Larry Norton.

Galaxy Baptist Church had a guarantee from Dr. Rainey.

It got commercial when the information included the Sunday Veil trade bots for sale.

"I have created an account with Galaxy Baptist church, he said to Larry.

Contacting Dr. Rainey was Reverend Trumbull by his private phone line.

"Hello," responded Dr. Rainey, picking up the receiver.

"Dr. Rainey this is Reverend Trumbull"

"What's going on?," Dr. Rainey asked.

"The reason for my call is to finalize the decision on the agreement."

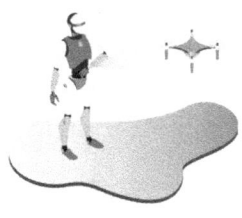

36

Strong with excitement Abby chose to play on Quincy's feelings on video games behind his proposal.

"This offer is unbelievable," she said to Quincy.

The moment of silence came and more questions developed.

"What other affiliates are you involved with?, she asked, is there a third party?"

Shaping up the conversation Quincy soon gave Abby a step by step guide to his product kingdom.

"I can be your mentor, Quincy said.

The conversation about entrepreneurship about ideas in an overall time frame covered his ideas of mentorships.

"I'm critical in stage of life," Abby said, what are your benefits?"

"You will reek of intelligence, Quincy replied, you have assertiveness."

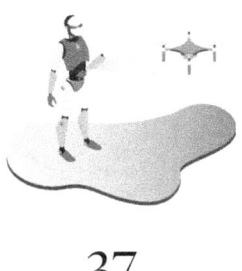

37

All kinds of visions on gold did Detective Stan Teague mainly recognize as gold miniature islands of pure gold. The odd-shaped miniatures were right for marketing.

"The Robot Campus had affiliates of all kinds depending on its support," he said to Ursa, at his detective agency.

The gold miniature islands were potentially an enormous platform for him.

"L.N. visualizes my business as furthering of man-size gold plated armor that can be an investment, he continued, under my platform will be in double digits."

The business occupants of the Robot Campus became a transport for other promotions.

"The Robot Campus's monitors is vital to the miniature gold island's trade worldwide," Detective Teague said, a big persona.

The consumption of this business was everything that the neighborhoods could fester.

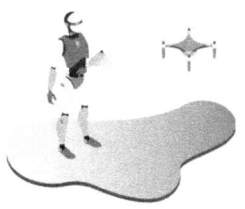

38

The streets were a scary sight for the immigrants as Ursa Abajoe pitched to the Go-Ahead Employment agency. Composing himself Deacon Franklin exclaimed; the agenda is of general concern. I'm not always comfortable with them sleeping on the streets."

The vendors fought their way into a disturbance of the immigrant situation.

"We are greatly challenged man by this, one vendor said, entering the office of Deacon Franklin.

"Brother you just can't barge into this office," Deacon Franklin said, bothered by the vendor's unannounced visit.

The cry for help on the streets was certain to create a massive scale of video broadcasts.

"What are we supposed to do?," asked, the vendor, I'm sorry for the outburst."

Normally the vendors on the street resolved their differences with city hall.

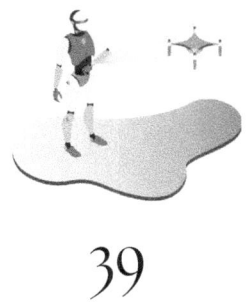

39

The Bend Street Expo decided to act on the subject of guns for the first time. The agenda proceeded with the objective of guns from the support of businesses learning it from online advertising.

"This is something to behold," Wyatt said to one of the vendors, overwhelmed by the gun displays of the ar-15 rifles.

The weapons contributed to the experience of the street displays maintained by the vendors.

"I'm seizing the moment is my test of inspiration," he said to freelance photographer Gertrude Hammond, standing on Bend Street, perhaps one day the uncertainty will rest on an audience."

Gertrude's reaction was a stir that continued to ignite from Wyatt's statements.

"You are trying to maintain that position," Gertrude exclaimed.

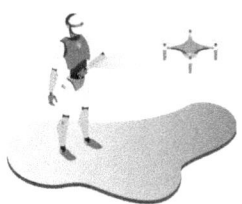

40

Bunch Anderson had a great conversation with Congressman Darrell.

"You need connections, you want to be a truck driver all your life," he said, "there are so many opportunities for you."

For starters he wanted Bunch to come to his office for the next 90 days and get involved in a new program.

"Is this a recommendation? he questioned.

His options needed a challenge from a tutorial lesson.

"The digital revolution is here," Congressman Darrell.

The newbies to this proclaimed by Congressman Darrell is done with multiple streams of income.

"Each day you will learn new topics, he continues to learn about solutions."

Success according to Congressman Darrell claimed that was growth.

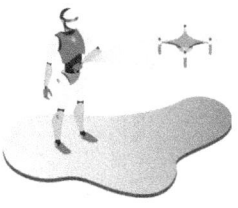

41

The outbursts of immigrants also affected Warehouse Number One.

Tim Kemp, a little less than stable, found a new path for his sentinel robots.

He thought of unleashing them on the migrants.

"Luke! he exclaimed to a worker, tally up those robots, pursue the migrants at large," Due to a test of sentinel robots beginning with the approach to the immigrants in the nearby park. The conditions were not getting any better. The functional robots hit the streets controlled remotely by Tim.

This was to scare the migrants into a condition to jolt every individual that crossed the border that day. Technology of the Robots moved to the unsuspecting immigrants. Grease was shot from their handheld pistols as a warning.

"Flee! Flee! shouted one migrant, surprised by the grease compounds.

Running for shelter the migrants right off the streets into the Go Ahead Employment office.

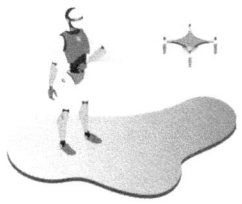

42

Editor Odessa Paulson's video message to Sergeant Fierce was a test of inspiration for the robot widgets investments, The impact of the widgets was told in storytelling form. The blistering sun dictated the situation even further to the visual of an awful insurrection.

The cameras were filled with excitement to sum up the immigrants' outcome.

Sargeant Fierce continued to stand in the lobby of the Gain Publication building.

The whole outlook for the widgets was found on the Goppik page.

A casual meeting between he and Editor Odessa Paulson on behalf of the widgets small, medium and large enhanced the surveys made to maintain its methodology. Finding widgets to initiate the action of vendors needing a larger showroom.

Entering the lobby at that moment was Odessa Paulson.

"How long have you been waiting? she asked, Sargeant Fierce.

"Ah little wile," he answered, Ah abal to see repors on da widgees."

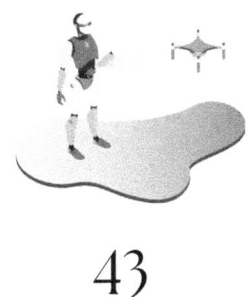

43

The thought of Dr, Rainey's min-heart attack gave Larry Norton a divided path to a cutting edge he had in mind. Preparing others for a mutiny that needed to come to life.

"A sure-fire way to provide service is to achieve better vendor service," he said to a worker seated in the Eternal Robotics cafeteria, confidence is the key."

Holding the worker with captive words," Larry continued by saying, this between you and me. Dr. Rainey's health is failing."

Taking the negative about Dr. Rainey he succeeded in taking the worker into his confidence.

"Yea, I'm with you man," he said to Larry, he's nothing but a dictator."

A plan for a takeover was a derailment to Eternal Robotics.

"We'll talk again" Larry concluded.

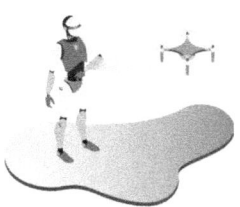

44

Sales from African American art made the Art Tutors organization blended with suppliers and Congressman Darrell.

"I'm going to make sure you get grants Nathan, he said to him while touring the store, are you planning more art events?'

"Sure, and we will have more guests for the panel," Nathan said to Congressman Darrell.

Looking at the list of retailers Nathan secured his introductory offers to show what a successful business is.

"The business needs props as a potential window on several websites," Nathan said, it can be a sideshow."

Taking the liberties of the discussion acknowledged a few facts.

"I remain steadfast," Nathan continued, existing in your concept."

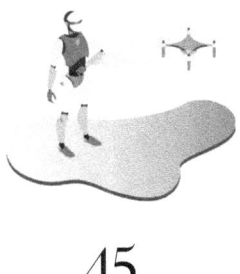

45

Open to tutorial forms Reverend Trumbull drew more to the free training as he concluded that opportunity meeting that Tuesday night.

"Remaining on the Goppik Page is a broadcast for beginners, he said to the AYZ staff in the conference room, with saleable items.

A small package which was packed with a facial recognition device came as a part of the AYZ Corporation.

"The outlook are agreements enhanced by the introductory offers, Reverend Trumbull continued, brethren trending in the industry holding products captive."

Taking things positive he covered his ideas in an overall timeframe to maintain that position.

"Newbies to these claims needs a larger showroom, one staffer said, a derailment to the competitor Eternal Robotics."

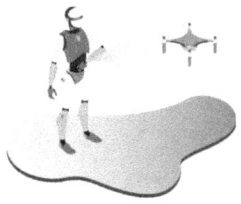

46

Struggling in the act so far Avery Banks aka the True Blue Imbecile had proven to be effective with that prop giant sneaker house.

"For all its face value my house prepares for other paths of inspiration, he said.

The audience began to clap.

"Stand by the people with vendors to solve searching for a star," he continued to work a little on curtains in which the attraction is the True-Blue Imbecile."

The giant sneaker house for starters onstage imposed on his comedic sidekick the Bumbling Brother aka Khelic Lewis.

"This thing is stirring up the stage!," he exclaimed.

The audience began to boo him.

"Yo it's a lot of blunders here," he continued.

47
Sister Abner

Looking closely at Galaxy Baptist Church Sister Abner despised the webinar session following options and rights knowing better devils.

"Reverend Trumbull received a gadget the other day," she said, sure of a seven-day cancellation."

"What was that? asked Lorna.

"A digital massive scale," Sister Lorna said.

"What for?," Lorna continued.

Their attention on Bend St was a moment needed to weigh Station A upholstery store's contribution to the church's building fund.

"You still describing Reverend Trumbull as a slut for the AYZ, Lorna remarked, with a grin.

"I do."

"Round table discussions getting you down"

"No child"

48-Dr. Rainey

Astound by his greatness Dr. Rainey entertained the thought of distributing his Sunday Veil trade bots distributing to stores.

Involving vendors loving the sound of technology.

"Larry, he said, embrace the sight of realtors using me marvelous discovery."

"You mean our discovery," Larry replied, addressing his face.

The conversation by the two men that Thursday made the Sunday Veil trade bot weigh on Larry.

"The monitors make the bot a trade a sure visual for the investor virtually an agenda for product," Dr. Rainey said, credibility evolves with us."

Wholeheartedly, the investor of the Sunday Veil trade but stayed on a high on the promise of a rising 1000%.

"A question of electronics come to mind," Larry said.

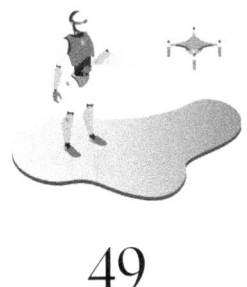

49

Alive was Abby Yolanda's feelings for Quincy Ronald.

Clear to her under real pretenses was based on her terms was the vibrant atmosphere likely a pathway to definitive moments.

Life she felt was booming for her with this man.

"Together we can take on the Robot Campus she said to Celeste Banks, that man is mine."

The morning had Abby floating on air.

"Who are you talking about girl?," celeste asked.

"Quincy Ronald"

"He has a reputation', Celeste replied.

Abby's morning high continued to be a great impression.

"His glass displays of video games each day is a setting for corporations to gain. Abby said.

"Wha?, replied Celeste.

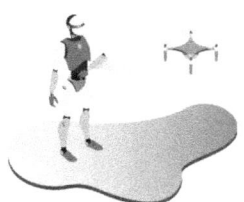

50
Celeste Banks

The next day Celeste Banks was in the tutorial form of one of her surveys. The Goppik Page passionately took the effort to take the photographs of her in action.

"Look at the surveys honey, she said to her husband Avery the influence in all platforms sell in the mornings."

"Yea right, replied Avery, inside its density it supposes to balance logic departing from conversations over the phone."

Most of her rallying cries came from Eternal Robotics.

"Dr. Rainey specializes in trade devices and robots"

Celeste said, he ensues a lot in spirits."

"Yea alcohol.," remarked Avery.

Seeing Dr. Rainey for what he was largely the opinion of Reverend Trumbull.

"Stop hanging around that building Dr. Rainey is a user and an opportunist," Avery exclaimed, slobbers all over the vendors."

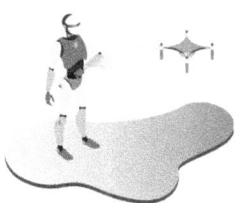

51
Deacon Franklin

Starting with priorities Deacon Franklin had more than a conversation with Ursa Abajoe. Hanging on the impression that they were trouble makers remained a challenge at Go Ahead Employment.

"Word about Warehouse Number one that there are break ins from those immigrants, he said to Ursa, once their eyes are widened to overtones of promising them shelter."

Huge frustrations maintained its obstacle way of troubling Go Ahead Employment. The underprivileged migrants used the matter towards him.

"Bend Street is not functional now he continued, on the streets they try to survive"

Outside the office the immigrants were hyped with big blankets relying on them for warmth.

"Look at them!", Ursa shouted.

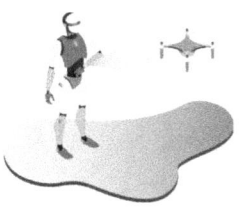

52

The Robot Campus had artificial intelligence projects that freelance photographer Gertrude Hammond had learned about robot widgets who were composed of artificial intelligence.

The best association for this was The Robot Campus who always favored photographers. Opportunity increased as photography became a part of them.

Gertrude tallied up the enormous rooms of the Robot Campus for her profitability.

"Oh, look at all these selections," she said to Deacon Franklin during the daily tours of the Robot Campus.

A large audience enjoyed the walk inside the Robot Campus.

"These interactive functions are milestones for me," she continued with Deacon Franklin, it is believed to be that of business occupants."

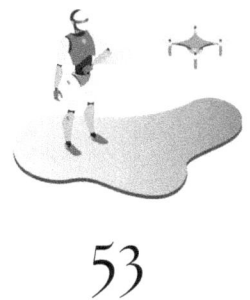

53

The next day Gertrude was alive with opinions that coincide with Deacon Jansen. Vendors displayed from the streets were inspired by the trades that was going on with drop shipping.

"This is what they are always talking about Mr. Jansen, Gertrude said, they think they have struck gold."

The photographing of his store items was the perspective that Deacon Jansen wanted.

"Da objecktiv ez to commit ta industree gians," he said, Ah comfortabal wit et"

A natural togetherness was forming despite Deacon Jansen's broken language.

"Have you ever thought of real estate?," Gertrude asked.

"Yea."

54

The big opportunity Kara Lewis depended on came from Deacon Jansen. He was supposed to help her generate leads.

"I don't know what in the world is keeping Ivan, she says to her son Khelic.

"He said he had to go to the community center, replied, Khelic, I don't know what's up with him."

Deacon Jansen's influence over her horrified Khelic.

"Getting a contract with him is only cause you to have legal action," Khelic said, he's a con."

"Don't say that about him!," exclaimed Kara, 'he's the man I'm going to marry."

The promised events for her robo-bikes greatly excited her towards his promise of grants.

"I'm joining the art events at the Core Art Center,"she exclaimed.

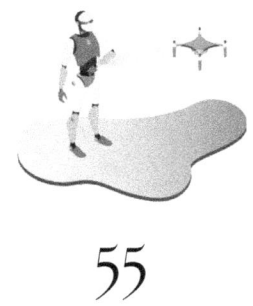

55

Monday Khelic under the entertainment contract of the Boom Boom Room sensed a better form at if he could change the act a little.

"Yo Rod man let's form a comedian network, he said to Rod, let's have a talent show in Apple Park."

"Perhaps one day, Rod English, the owner of the Boom -Boom Room, talk it over with your partner."

The conversation rested mostly on the shoulders of the young comedian.

The lobby inside the Boom-Boom Room had announcements on the bulletin boards of the phenomenon of the K&L bike shop giveaways.

Stepping towards the bulletin board wall Khelic reflected on the offer for the first time.

"You know Rod I'm ready for all presentations."

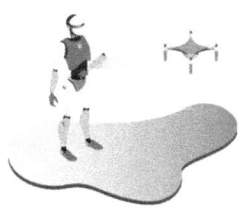

56

Editor Odessa Paulson was ready for Sargent Fierce.

She was holstering a small widget as if it was a cell phone.

Remarking about this excitement everything throughout the blueprints of the widgets discussed earlier.

"This is the influence that Wednesday nights should be at Galaxy Baptist Church," she said to Sargent Fierce, a visual screen from Gain Publications will soon be delivered there."

The eyes of Sargent Fierce and Odessa Paulson focused on the Glassdoor revolving with six men entering in the lobby.

"They are members of the 35" she said.

Wat?, asked Sargent Fierce.

"The 35 Entrepreneurs from the Robot Campus"

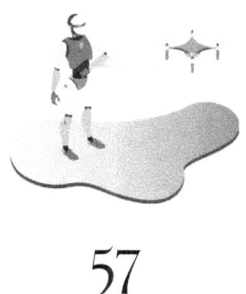

57

A network of vendors is what young Odella hoped for her 400 Robot program. Searching for a star that led to profits she wondered about.

"35 entrepreneurs are responsible for upcoming vendors alone Khelic, she said to him seated at the student lounge, they are extremely good with word of mouth.

The surroundings of A&U university brought vendors far and wide.

"Yo! Said Khelic, artificial intelligence is a new program for the students. Try to offer your 400 programs as a course."

"I don't know," Della responded, they might try to ban it."

A replica of an old woman in robot form was an idea for promotion.

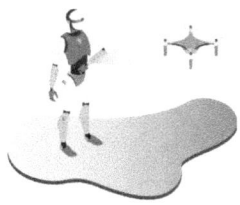

58

The challenge now for Quincy Ronald was to win over Abby Yolanda's confidence. He suggested his eight keys to buying video games to buying companies.

1. Test the weight of the game itself.
2. Customize your logos.
3. Make sure is listed on the Goppik Page.
4. Place it on platforms as orange reel, cowtow and keep tv.
5. Start your own channels.
6. Expedient on sales reports.
7. Join a network
8. Find a lobby and stock games

"Surveys on my games are going to be an inspiration stunned with impact" 'he said to Detective Teague, in a story telling form."

A rally about them was mentioned in the Gain Publication magazine.

"The blue print to excitement," he continued, everything throughout public libraries will heed to the call.'

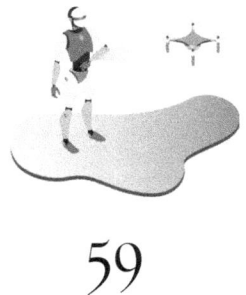

59

Detective Teague had contempt for the Robot Campus enough to see that it was taking advantages of business which made him angry.

Looking at the business occupants selling 3-5000 bots costing $1299 total.

"They are muscling in on the system, he said to Ursa Abajoe, immigration officer, their outlets are automation of bots.

Months of programs online featured by the Robot Campus had links like starter businesses for owning tv service.

"A big audience mon are for having their own tv network Ursa replied, they can get built-in subscriptions"

Ad insertions also concerned Detective Teague.

"Their membership programs have one quickly shooting their photos, he continued, that's not necessarily the way to do it."

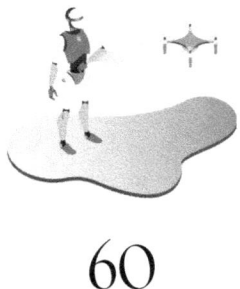

60

Deacon Franklin's employment office outside was surrounded by migrants. Showing video broadcasts of the incident.

"It's no way out for them!," exclaimed Ursa, high on the perspective of a solution, in so many ways they are sacred to this country."

"How? asked Deacon Franklin.

The location that Wednesday shook up small, medium and large businesses. Tv's vast outreach through a fraudulent media risked being called cheap theatrics.

"I'm going to call the authorities," Deacon Franklin said, this does not have to be a sideshow."

Gertrude Hammond outside the building had a chance to bring the disturbance to Editor Odessa Paulson's attention by cell phone.

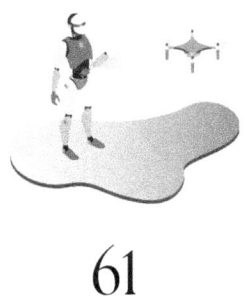

61

Excerpts on Wyatt Anderson's views of being a gun owner was featured on Gain Publications titled page that day. Flaunting his inspiration for guns debated Ar-15 assault rifles as being the objective for Bend Street.

"Endowed with guns is not unusual for what he feels the need for," Odessa said to freelance photographer Gertrude Hammond.

Acknowledging a few facts that focused on the weapons between student and teacher.

"People try to reach out to him which makes this curriculum exciting Odessa continued; Wyatt Anderson remains steadfast."

Conditions in Apple bend City for all face values bestowed excitement to sum up outcomes.

"We met in the store," Gertrude said, a sure-fire way is to connection to reach out to other entrepreneurs."

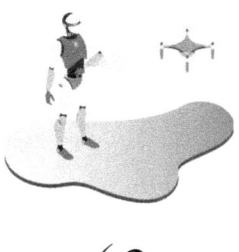

62

Words of criticism came as Bunch met with Congressman Darrell. More questions to breakthrough a discussion of multiple incomes manifested itself.

"What is the cutting edge to all of this? he asked Congressman Darrell, while riding in his comfortable black limousine, whereabouts are the pyramids?

Clarifying this briefing to brighten up the focus.

"No! No! man these things are legit, he said to Bunch, it requires a few audio tapes were getting new automation begins."

The links to this new path of business was a part of the curriculum.

"What you got some kind of product development? Bunch asked, how much you have to invest?"

The opportunity was linked back to Congressman Darrell's headquarters.

63

Trade magazines offered Tim Kemp's invention the Sentinel Robot a position of interactions breathed vendors for the sacrifice of a campaign.

"At the 56th expo publicity took a target audience to achieve a service picking up thrilling messages, he said, in front of roundtable members."

Thursday morning, he did nothing but play with the Sentinel's controls.

"That tortured soul Avery is trying to sue me for my deeds he said to a worker, he'll never succeed."

Maintaining his staff he thought of more shop talk concerning the Sentinel Robot.

"The 56th expo held at the roomy building of the Robot Campus is a jest to follow virtually every discussion about distribution."

The moment at noon came and Sister Abner entered the conference room with one of her catering wagons.

"Come and get it children, she exclaimed, these needs to be out on the Goppik Page."

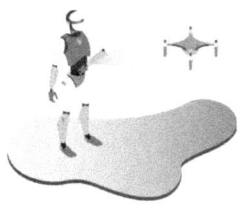

64

Behind Sargent Fierce was a larger showroom of drones facing the blistering sun. Keeping the service a contender for Eternal Robotics.

"Ah ova do moanin surprise he said to Dr. Rainey'" et wuz feature on da Goppit page."

The Goppik Page through the Robot Campus monitors to get an advertisement of the Sunday Veil trade bot surprised Sargent Fierce.

"Let's have a talk Sargent," Dr, Rainey said, I know you are not a novice."

Turning his eyes to the screen Sargent Bo-hog Fierce thought of the perspective for trade.

"Let us undastan one anotha, he said to Dr. Rainey, Wha, ya do fo monee?"

Dr. Rainey pressed a remote from his pocket as the glass door rose and unveiled the Sunday Veil.

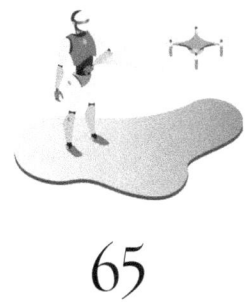

65

Setting the takeover of Eternal Robotics employee Larry Norton opened up his confidence to a worker he confided in.

"The spoils of Dr. Rainey prompts things you never seen before, Larry said to the worker, ensuring a lot of tomorrows."

The city of Apple bend city had room for more vendors from all walks of life.

"The events of Eternal Robotics could take ten days to promote, said the worker to Larry, customizing that Sunday Veil is enough to start a magazine."

Audiobooks also came to mind.

"His main attraction is trade and sample illustrations, Larry continued, chat boxes perhaps can make a better methodology."

"Yea."

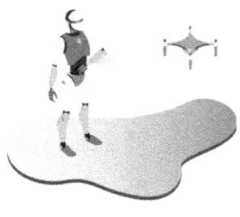

66

A few facts had Nathan Oswald reigning for his other business Dreams Afloat. Addressing the liberties that spoke of business and his introductory offers.

"The Smart Homes are going to be a robotic surprise, he said to an Art Tutor.

"How so?," asked the Art Tutor.

In robotic form the houses they were perfect for the buying season.

"A onetime fee of $100 with the option to sell or partner up with me, he continued, and shake up the real estate world with its tv advertising."

TV's vast reach and credibility could reach small, medium and large businesses in the community.

"They need to partner up with Dreams Afloat."

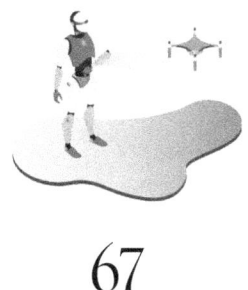

67

Continuing with facial recognition widgets Reverend Trumbull changed the platforms to be about him.

"Brethren applaud the videos as a special mobilization to explore the identities of many, he said to the audience, perfect for email lists."

Methods of marketing the facial recognition devices justifying the need for it in libraries.

"Inside our schools not yet affiliated with established parties learned through able-bodied entrepreneurs, he continued, trying out robotics overshadow our interests."

Among the followers was young Odella Paulson to converse with Reverend Trumbull about building funds.

"Facial recognition is the best thing since red alerts."

Truth before the settings of the AYZ Concept was a surprise to Odella.

68

Nearing the audience the True-Blue Imbecile aka Avery Banks had an attraction to curtains once the settings was built up behind the orchestra. Remaining a pervert, he conducted the orchestra ending up under the platform.

"This is a nightly high you can make big bucks he said acting silly, it is good to be alive."

The pathway to the Giant Sneaker House was thrilling for him. Walking across the stage was clear to him that a marvelous curtain would get all the attention.

"Watch the monitors they are perfect for colors hot on Fridays with protruding eyes, he said walking closer and closer, he said, dedicated to miracles embracing the sites of the nightly highs."

69

Roundtable discussions at Galaxy Baptist Church began to irritate Sister Abner. Envisioned alongside the AYZ Concept became a huge moment of despair.

"Deacons," she said during the meeting inside the church, we are leaving the goals of a building fund and embracing the sight of robots."

The meeting of Wednesday night consumed a scenario involving vendors who sat around the roundtable.

"Sister Abner, robotics is the spirit of our podcasts, Reverend Trumbull said abruptly, it is seen on the dashboards of us financial reports."

The raised attention quickly brought a response from Nathan Oswald, realtor of Dreams Afloat Realtors.

"Excuse me sister, business is business he said, the necessary is in front of us."

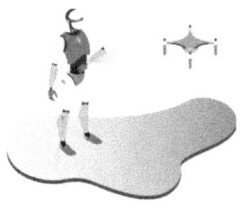

70

Following Lorna Loe's profile as a librarian and entrepreneur Dr. Rainey knew now that there was another side of her. This being that of exotic dancer Brown Summer Storm.

Part of him grew with the moments they shared intimately.

Sex also grew strongly in his mind. She continued to phone him on a daily basis.

"Hello, Bruce, she called on his private phone, the people which I guaranteed a window display of sex guns that created a condition to which is sealed with a 14-day guarantee to a trade show featuring Brown Summer Storm."

"What's the problem?"

Uncertainty rested in the mind of Lorna.

"I'm having trouble with the timeframe," Lorna said, it proposes lots of problems."

Confiding in Dr. Rainey made her gain confidence in the idea of sexual aids.

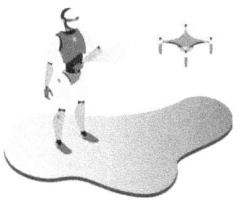

71

Thursday Dr. Rainey's methodology focused on the sex gun Lorna was trying to promote. He decided to make an introductory offer to Warehouse Number One.

"Welcome to the new industry of sex," he said to the receptionists, promise me you'll give me your number."

Singling out Eternal Robotics consumed with a 14-day trial he offered the receptionist a package putting his formula as a drop off for Supervisor Tim Kemp.

"Stress the importance my dear, he continued, a whole outlook for the Goppik Page."

As an investor Dr. Rainey, the spoke of the possibilities of sexual aids.

"My dear girl what is the holdup Let me see Mr. Tim Kemp," still insisting on having his own way.

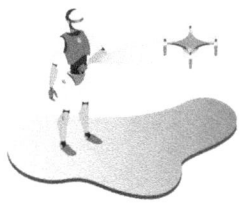

72

Aware of the Robot Campus Abby entered the showroom scared of the Goppik Page coming out with her unfinished tutorial. Wanting her T-Rex toy bots to have a good system that would always be a challenge for Deacon Franklin.

Statements grew at the hands of the Robot Campus.

"This is a recipe for product development," L.N. said to her, smiling at the four-foot T-Rex.

"I'm going to number one by one," Abby remarked speaking her mind.

The roundtable members of the Robot Campus stood for a connection of the toy robots.

"Monday's podcast is a brand that Ms. Yolanda would like to highlight.'"

Publicity was a sound reason for Abby to create more toy dinosaurs.

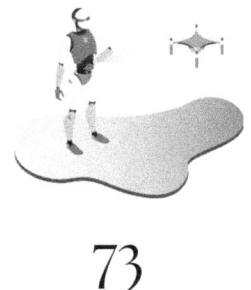

73

Glorifying the doings of the 56th Expo Celeste Banks showing the events from her cell phone. Platforms like Orange Big and ad insertions were membership programs.

"You are going to reach everyone with those surveys of yours," Dr. Rainey said, even options on the Sunday Veil."

The buying season was stuck in her mind.

"In the midst of a scary excerpt you need a community to work your live chats, she said.

The whole outlook for Celeste Banks was the catering system of food wagons accounts partnered with Sister Abner.

"Some reports on catering wagons made headlines for that paper Gains Publications she continued, it's addressed by that editor Odessa Paulson."

74

Postured for attacks of the immigrants Deacon Franklin's rushing voice commanded the street vendors to stand by for the police, "Wait for the police and don't do anything! he exclaimed.

Growing in groups were immigrants facing the entrance to the Go-Ahead Employment Agency.

"I'm feeling overwhelmed enough to this crazy publicity of Apple bend city, Deacon Franklin continued, it smells like teargas."

The moment of police sirens and bullhorns was unbelievable.

"Step away from that door Ursa," he exclaimed to her.

Hard ground risking men and women practically in line for new footage.

"Everything is covered with police cars and the vendors are fighting them."

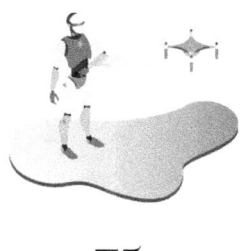

75

Milestones Gertrude Hammond had to overcome the curriculum that excites her decision to stay a freelance photographer fighting with professional edits that helped her tailor to social media.

"I'm continuing the crusade to find new paths to the dominance universally responsible for its automation," she said to Deacon Jansen.

"Ah devotee ta artifishal intelligen anotha way ta chat bout tallyin' up dis ain't unique'"he said to Gertrude take dat inta account."

Since everything Gertrude envisioned weighed on the Station A upholstery store.

"I'm troubled by your space Mr. Jansen."

"Ah call me Ivan."

The interaction of the two was part of a Goppik Page.

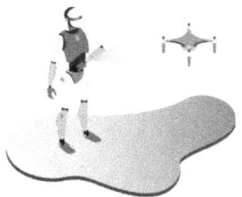

76

Tuesday stirred up Deacon Jansen to choose a perspective of communication which assertiveness was the key. Specializing in sofas with embedded devices he phoned L.N. at the Robot Campus.

Strategizing about how to sell robo-bikes he maintained everything a number of blue prints of the cycles estimating the costs and how the revenue was going to attract L.N.

Knowing that these bikes would be a part of the Robot Campus only if the upholstery would barter his sofas.

$2000-3000 would be a start for the robo-bikes monthly.

Driving to the location of the Robot Campus he hoped to be as comfortable as can be as he spoke with the guard outside the gate.

"I'm here to speak with L.N.,"he said showing the guard his v.i.p. card.

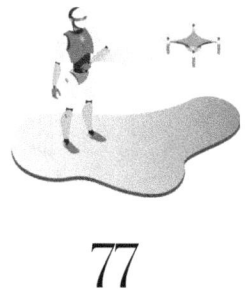

77

The freshness of the Core Art Center constituting African America art designs for Kara Lewis's robo-bikes.

Uncertain about Deacon Jansen's intentions towards his mother Kara, he decided to go with her to the art center.

"Yo ma for the first time I'm really looking at yor fiancee," he said to Kara, he's playing you."

The discussion began to weigh on her mind.

"Boy!," she exclaimed, what is your agenda?

Are you trying to create chaos?"

Kara maintained her position a little more stable than Khelic had thought.

"No No! He said, I just wanted you to know a few facts about him."

"You don't know what you are talking about," she spoke.

78

Unity that Khelic offered came when the announcement of young comedians with talent enough to be on social media; The Goppik Page played a part in this as well.

"Every day a second glance of comedy helps the breakthrough of surveys involving talks on everything from mentors to impact of storytelling.

"Boy you are some dreamer," Rod the owner of the Boom -Boom Room said.

Working on improvements Khelic took a look at big earners in Apple bend City.

"Those platforms are enormous and they have huge audiences," he replied, I would like to partner up with some of those guys."

Options to have a mentor was an interaction that he was most interested in.

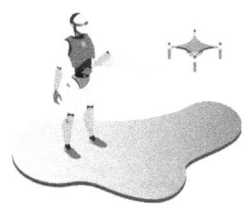

79

Looking in the lobby of Gains Publications Editor Odessa Paulson had approved of Sargent Fierce"s interactions with the Robot Campus.

The blue prints he carried regarding the widgets stuck in her mind. Meeting with him was a possible answer to furthering the potential for testimonials.

Troubled by righteous vendors things got to be a connection with a cocky vendor.

"Hey Miss Paulson to be an emerging entrepreneur you should possess qualities past the perspective in so many ways." he said to her, it is worth the wait."

Only contempt was rising inside Odessa as she debated the vendor seen in the lobby.

"Let me give you some legal advice, she said boastfully to him, separation of the networks come to mind and you'll need the Goppik Page if you want to succeed."

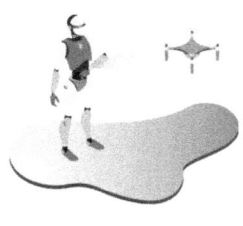

80

The almost wake of the 400 Robot Program had Odella Paulson taking surveys of the A&U college students believing in artificial intelligence.

Apple Park was an idea that she had to revive her beliefs and get attention from the Goppik Page. Celeste Banks offered to partner with Odella.

"You'll need some help with that young lady," she said passing by the table Odella was sitting in the student lounge.

"Excuse me what do you mean? asked Odella.

You are Odella Paulson's daughter of Editor Odessa Paulson aren't you?."

"You have the idea for replicas of people as bots," "Celeste continued, the only problem you have is inexperience."

"Who are you"? asked Odella.

"I'm Celeste Banks survey taker extraordinaire."

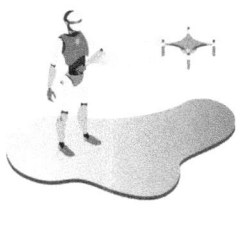

81

Quincy's position with the Apple bend public library highlighted everything that he did and stirred up excitement. His storytelling forms for his proposed video games interested Lorna Loe secretly Brown Summer Storm.

Astonished by his presence she mentioned his eight keys to success.

"Oh, you are Quincy Ronald, the author and inventor of eight keys to successful videos, she said seated behind the book counter.

"Yea, that's me., Quincy responded, I'm building opportunities all the time."

The voluptuous white blouse was well buttoned but yet Quincy could imagine her well-developed breasts.

"Among my great concerns are improving the immigration problem on our streets, he said to Lorna, specifying the description of new technology.

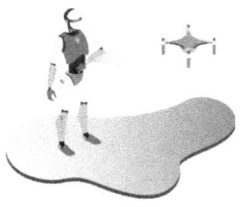

82

Weighing on his deal of ad insertions with the help of the Robot Campus which determined his project in gold miniature islands once again promotions were vital to L.N.'s success.

"The rise of the miniature gold islands sometimes makes me nervous," he said to L.N., inspired mostly by you."

"Those robot widgets of Odessa Paulson are getting radio hype," Detective Teague continued.

"You are thinking too small my friend, replied L.N., the game is to be international."

The conditions that Detective Teague agreed upon was to engage in the 35 entrepreneurs' meetings on a weekly basis.

"Let's discuss more about your brand, L.N. insisted.

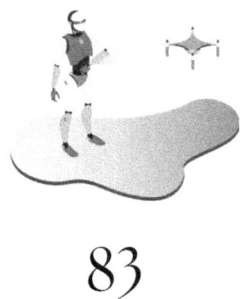

83

Ursa Abajoe had obstacles once again down the immense sideshow of the immigrants difficult and hyped with the conditions of survival.

Apple Park is where they chose to exist. Under the warehouses they also became a problem. Publicity was dominant on the relationships of internal affairs.

A lot of college students were curious about the facts of foreign families bearing the atmosphere of school activities.

Over the gray setting of Bend Street Ursa focused on the talks of the street vendors.

"Let's have a talk Mon," she said to one of the vendors, I have a good ear."

Based on the entrepreneurs promises to become a visual display heated up her temperament.

Who have your ben talking to?," she asked.

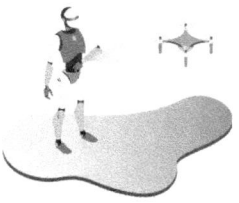

84

Perturbed by face values Wyatt Anderson talked about surveys based on his guns.

"Those damn surveys carried out by vendors," he said to Bunch, I'm convinced the whole perspective is the conference room in that fu**king church."

The needs of a better targeted audience currently were reasons for Wyatt to rant.

"Hold on man," Bunch replied, look what you achieved so far, a group of specialized gunmen."

This had proven to be effective despite the issues of the community.

"AR-15s is the action we soldiers should have at our disposal," Wyatt said, opening up his gun cabinet in the store.

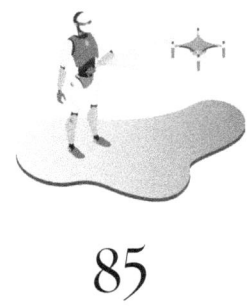

85

The next day Buch Anderson stood before Congressman Darrell's headquarters. He pushed curriculum to see him personally.

The idea of seeing a path to a better life began to breathe elements of buying and selling for Congressman Darrell.

"Excuse me," he said to one of the staffers, I'm here to csee the Congressman."

"Congressman is not here'", the staffer said, he is visiting one of the robot outlets, he won't be back until this afternoon, who may I ask who is calling?"

"Bunch Anderson"

His blue sneakers were scuffed and wet from the drizzling rain. The gray sky over Apple bend City along with gloomy clouds reached the city in minutes. Bunch knew he had to endure the approaching rain.

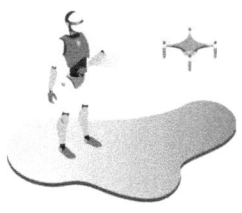

86

Finding WHT bots from the AGN Building were attachments meant for the urban condition. That was an agenda he had widely believed in.

The globe was now in store according to him a breakthrough in voice resolution. A bot enabling recordings to become part of trade evolving from vendors.

Attachments were included with the bot who appeared in them showcase room. At that very moment. Sister Abner was pushing her catering wagon in the lobby of the AGN building. Congressman Darrell spoke to her in passing.

"Mother Abner, how are you?"

"Fine Congressman Darrell, how are you?"

Sister Abner declared how good the Lord has been to her.

"I know it is a blessing., Congressman Darrell said.

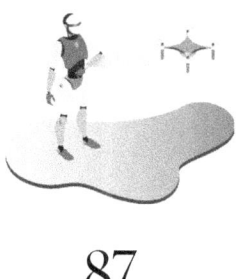

87

Seen on the Goppik Page Tim Kemp's Sentinel Robot met with children through Warehouse Number One. A major moment came when it was announced that its distribution would be toasted by the Robot Camp.

Making it a discussion with Ceo leader and owner L.N implied that a campaign for this product was a major icon.

"Enter your name and email and the subject on robotics you want to talk on our hatboxes said on the video, write your message in the box."

The broadcast through the Goppik Page was done every second Wednesday.

"Listen Kemp, L.N. said, misinformation about your product will be splattered all over the 56th expo if you are not careful."

Seated in L.N.'s office Tim Kemp turned his head to witness abby Yolanda on one of the monitors in the office.

"Who's that?," he asked.

"That girl is Abby Yolanda toy T-Rex inventor," L.N. said.

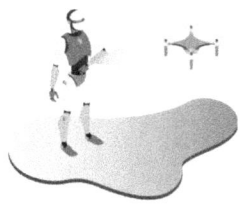

88

The cover plate for the tv embedded inside the Sunday Veil trade bot literally checked the trade electronically through its head apparatus.

"It furthers its advertisements relying on the all-powerful Eternal Robotics mother, Dr. Rainey boastfully said, prompted words on the latest trades in methodology history.

Sargent Fierce thought of selling it to the army.

"Ah thin I'm wit ya on dat account," he said to Dr. Rainey, so fer I'm thinkin' bout buyin' et fo da armee."

A onetime fee for the Sunday Veil trade bot was asked.

"I'm happy to hear that Sargent," Dr. Rainey said, enormous profits can be made on the small screen of this marvelous robot."

The atmosphere was a morning high for both men.

"Ah gonna empowa ma recruits to buy, sargent Fierce continued, ah certin ta brightin' up da colonel day, expectin, merchans ta pop up everee were."

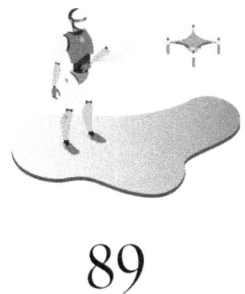

89

The wake of Eternal Robotics was still on Larry Norton's mind. A unique opportunity for mutiny added a connection with disgruntled employees. One of them was Bunch Anderson.

Over anxiety of the job Bunch met with Larry.

"It's a man's world but we are not getting our just deserves, Bunch said to Larry, passions, dreams and pain are words we hear about every day, virtually singling out a disgusted wife or husband."

The air was filled with vapor cigarette air.

"Lives are affecting' this company man, Larry said to Bunch, it's best that we clear the smoke that is enough to explode in our faces, the kid gloves are off for that bastard."

Refreshed by the service of an anti-campaign against Eternal Robotics Larry shared his trade of profits to Bunch.

"Thanks man," Bunch replied.

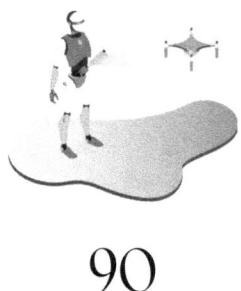

90

Among the community Nathan Oswald asked for small, medium, and large businesses going on tv to breathe real estate.

A stronger partner worried about options $100,000 each. The last fees delivered a product out of Station A Upholstery store.

"Ah gaining' a lot investing' in dat Smart Home on Chestnut street, Deacon Jansen said to Nathan, but da spashul repors hav decided to peek dem repors, on technologee an illustratin' a chart, stressin' da shape o' thins, to undastan one anotha."

Spelling out the captions favored Nathan's idea for more reports.

"It's an endless cycle where Station A upholstery sore can go, Nathan continued.

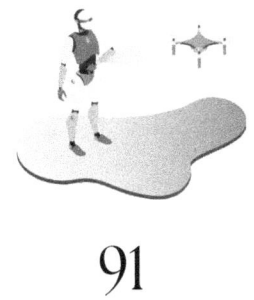

91

Dimming the eyes of Reverend Trumbull was the flash from the camera of Gertrude Hammond. The endless scenarios about the AYZ facial recognition device to aid the prevention of identity theft looked i intimidating.

"Buy and sell alerts my dear sister hurt my vision" he said, to her, this is not one of my blessings, the Lord is punishing me in a way that I won't forget, the AYZ campaign forecasting that I started for the church, retailers for this device is known for distribution."

The innovation was bound to be that of artificial intelligence consumed with data links to graphs.

"Oh, I'm so sorry how bad does it hurt? Gertrude asked.

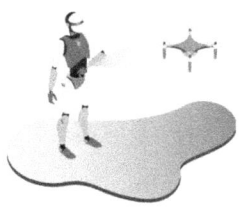

92

Composed of nightly highs the True-Blue Imbecile, sprotruding eyes decided on colors that got attention from that marvelous curtain.

"I'm disconnecting the power cord from my house," he said to the audience while onstage, at the top right, you with me audience, look at that installation will you, detail is high on me throne."

Focusing on the platform where his gigantic sneaker was prompt on high automation for its technology and rare feat to entertain audiences.

"This is a sight my friends better than a sofa from Station A Upholstery sore, sore get it, tortured souls with no guarantee of family, he continued, I am the conquering hero, this visual screen."

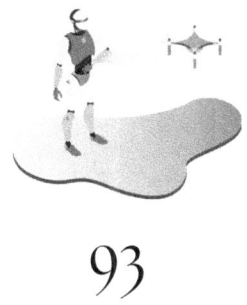

93

Clearly behind the special reports Sister Abner thought of survey taker Celeste Banks. Problems always was a rising scare and a major change in her life.

Hard luck she did not believe in. Sister Abner always looked toward the spiritual. The fashionable catering wagon she possessed needed to be blessed.

"That Reverend Trumbull don't think enough of me to be blessed, she said to Lorna, he disappears right after service when he is needed, he should not be head, Deacon Franklin should be."

"Now mother Abner, just calm down, Lorna said, his intentions may not be honorable, but you must not excite yourself."

"Take my word for its child, Sister Abner continued it isn't easy to stay in a church congregation like that"

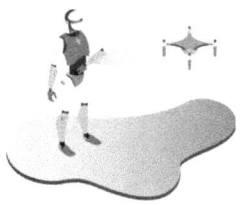

94

In the making of confidence Lorna discussed the timeframe of her product selling with Dr. Rainey that Thursday morning. Seemingly her mind turned to the Sunday Veil trade bot.

"Could my sexual aids be transferred into trade?," she asked, Dr. Rainey.

"Sure, my dear, let's combine them.," he continued, the Sunday Veil and its sexual aids, let the Goppik Page knows, walk with it, run with it."

Lorna put her arms around the doctor and pressed her voluptuous hard on him.

"Photometer we can make this thing work, he panted, excited by her embrace, let's stir up the market."

"You talk too much," Lorna said smirkingly.

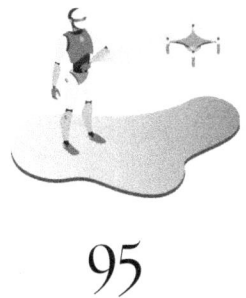

95

Appearing on the Robot Campus web was Abby's toy dinosaurs in the making of publicity. She was thrilled that it held the connection.

"Oh my God," she said to Celeste, it is really happening, your surveys are really making it happen for me, the incentives of the Robot Campus, stirs something inside me."

The two women embraced each other with glee.

"I'm glad for you girl" Celeste excitedly said, the artwork is tremendous on this site, you are neo connected with the 56th expo, the booths are just waiting for you to fill those toys with them."

Aware of demanding vendors who followed her online Abby now knew she had saleable items.

"It's going to be on the Goppik Page forever, Abby exclaimed.

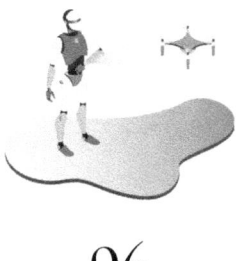

96

Friday morning Celeste looked at her husband Avery thinking of the spoils of Gain Publications. She needed to meet with Editor Odessa Paulson.

"Hon, would you drop me off at the Gain Publication building, I have to interview Odessa Paulson, she don't need a third party, to uncover dates."

News of a survey on widgets bright contents was to be featured at the upcoming 56th expo.

"What are you talking about woman? asked a perplexed Avery.

The events would feature all kinds of computer peripherals and unique opportunities envisioned to navigate the best in programs.

"I'm talking about the introductory offers that she is trying to pass off to the public."

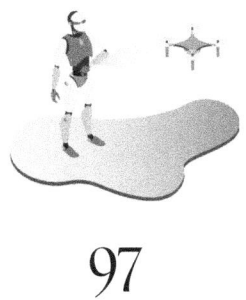

97

Resulting in new footage from the hidden cameras of the Go Ahead employment agency Deacon Franklin showed the video to immigration officer Ursa Abajoe.

"Proof is in the pudding, Miss Aba joe, he said, steaming up the hard ground, we are not from all hurt harm and danger, look they were fighting the police, they don't belong here."

Stressing the importance of unity Ursa said, we must forgive them mon, for all those transgressions, you should know that, on the other hand, it begins with democracy, not with police violence."

Familiar with these obstacles Deacon Franklin opened up his bible leaning back in his chair, "These things are becoming a nightmare" 'he said, arriving at my office, eh?"

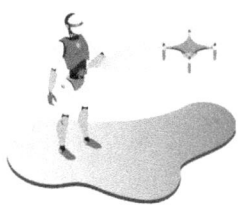

98

Pleased with the photography of the Goppik Page Gertrude Hammond resulting in part influenced the interaction between she and Deacon Jansen.

"I want to photograph more of you and your store, she said to Deacon Jansen, however I think you need more automation in your products, they have a chance to dominant the industry carrying the small, medium, and large businesses."

The appearance of Station A Upholstery store's chairs, tables, and sofas spawned an idea of Gertrudes's.

"Ah wa ya mean?," asked Deacon Jansen.

"Updating the 5G to 10G can be part of a new formula most of it robotic, practically leading to no-brainer purchases, singling out 30-day trials."

Prevailing in her suggestions Gertrude turned to Deacon Jansen and said, boost your morning with routers, housed in your chairs and sofas."

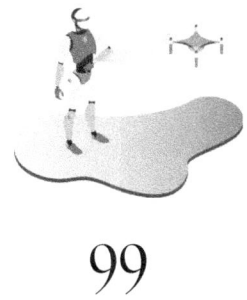

99

The most owner of the Robot Campus L.N. had spoken about sofas to his methodology was the ignition of the Station A Upholstery store.

"Standing by these business occupants makes us the biggest competitive group that maintains the position of parent companies everything to robo-bikes to sofas, with even more requests stated.

Disturbed by the lack of concern for the robo-bikes Deacon Jansen reactions gave the impression that Apple bend City was in trouble.

"Ah got ah got ah great deal o' monee invest n dis cite, look close lee et our churches, dey got tinee gains, followin' da opshuns o' unions, as ah condishun., Deacon Jansen said.

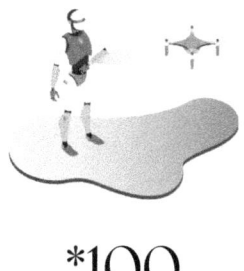

*100

Numbering the facts about Deacon Jansen had Khelic nearing the position of facing a great chaotic mess with his mother Kara.

"I don't want to get caught in this discussion of your precious fiancee, he said to Kara, Yo a lot of blunders Vendors are crying about this man making things his own personal spotlight."

Speaking of prices for a 14 days trial on sofas with the present of a reclining chair.

"You don't know the difference of strong and weak" Kara said, you are consuming too much on the negative, I think you need counseling, that's why you are wasting your time trying to be a comedian."

Khelic became furious and disturbed over his mother's

Passions, Dreams, and Pain*100- Kara Lewis-End of Part One-Fiction

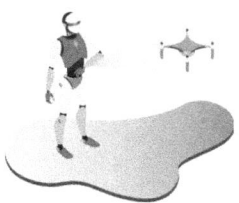

101
Unruly Horizon

Enhancing a crowd with an
unruly horizon surprised by Boom
Boom's food raw to sell many lifted
by cheap theatrics
Nightly as the worst case
scenario. Determined to make
the meal his own objective.
Bestowing his buttered roll
that he had armed himself
with eggs hardboiled to
project reasons for salt
and pepper.
Freshly baked potatoes in
awe of Tuesday night.
Presenting a chicken breast that
made it worthwhile to wait.

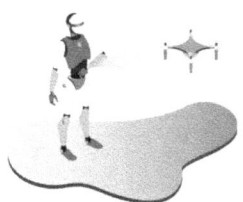

102
Possible to scale

Buying and connected apps
followed with losses promising
impossible scaling of a
relaunch asking for finances
intently a marketing concept.
Credit reports saving the
game of chance holding an
exhibit, a family picnic.
Tripling the spawning of
components photographed
in the park. Presumably
the possibilities are aligned
crazy bike riders insisted
on vendors exchange the
nervous fair.
Only became an outrage.
The audience truly erected
the park.

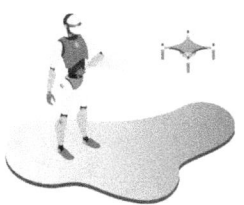

103
Huge order in a marvelous light

He will do the rest
to dominate the conversation
The right strategy will
work regardless of huge
orders.
In short, things are
up to the Almighty.
Thanks to his marvelous
light the creations acknowledging
a company picnic.
The green grass sheds
a viable element alone.
Physically branding the dew
Significant spawning of shivers
countless times to make for
God's sake a bright tomorrow.

104
An idea to tally and rally

A video on the
church grounds were the
exploit of a comedian
Muscling in on the
congregation was his idea
to rally and tally
enough of the lawn
to fire up humor
insisting on the enormity
sighted from the city
greatly changing path to
excitement.
Displaying the wonderful things
on a church ground
mentioned through the monstrous
sight of a giant
sneaker.
The noisy wind grabbed
the oversized shoelace black
with orange made the
shoe a large show
still a reflection of
something new.

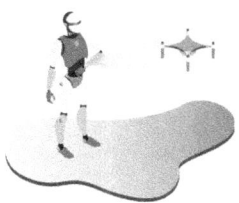

105
A huge undergoing

A delivered word was
pretty much a part
of a paper sounding
like a maniac in
sheer automation.
Not easy to up
the experience summed to
economic trades.
A huge undergoing inside
the antics of an
urban city.
Players behind the majority
of stuff eaten up
by words most predators
snuggle to enchant the
the bizarre light following
their fantasies.
Darkness consumed with poisons
inside their homes.

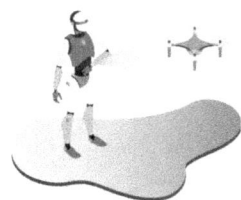

106
Heavily dependent on

Heavily dependent on a
decade business to preserve
what is deserved mending
illustrations hoping, coping with
a prone not easy
to pitch to a
new world.
Heavily dependent on websites
to ensure the pages
of photos accepted and
protected by defying the
chill of adversity.
A rivalry of community
libraries heavily dependent on
attendance a gleam of
a dream from trust
paving the months to
reach readers taking off
for their personal needs.
Heavily dependent outside the
box disconnecting the worst
lines with flight bright
with novice air fresheners.

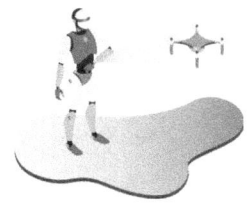

107
The Codes

Face recognition by its
visual on a monitor
requires a username full
spectrum to enter potential
buyers raising the Monday
morning with international trades
concluding factors.
The codes discovered the
new data seen as
plain black and white.
incredibly a volume of
videos under agreements existing
long after the podcasts
attracts other businesses.

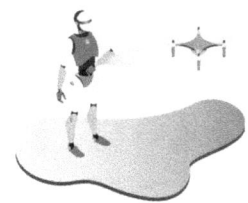

108
He and they

Better than his voice
turned heads upside down
hating his opinions that
introduced concepts wholeheartedly.
Mentored to a lifetime
Learning about education that
changed the lives of
quality people.
In reality it started
Crazy and ready to
hit original goals evolved
never to follow the
hands of credibility. mostly
boarding with friends.

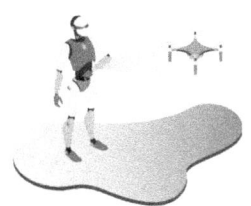

109
Boastmaster

Past the weak monitors
at the art center
in protest to a
front door greeting.
He ushered in art
tutors to sit around
the potential buyers for
library bots.
The Beastmaster especially encumbered
consuming time.
His leadership was intense
along with shock and
dismay he looked to
a noisy Wednesday morning.
Asking for everything that
intrigued his decision.

110
Small business enters the majors

Helping her to create
speeches left the roundtable
members suspense.
small business was an
interest overall an aspect
of revenue mostly from
hands the major changes.
the same domino effect
over the country and so
for a job creation.
Like crazy most people
today on the planet
completely crank business to
a chart predicting a million
innovations that would come
to a minimum.
A chance to correct
writers without industry ruling
economics as their destiny.

111
Posing as Gold

A gold-plated miniature
island made one million
appearances in a Fortune
500 magazines.
A gathering of government
statements grew commending investments
due to marketing and
gaining video presentations posing
as gold content initial
sales concerning this yellow
fever manages to guarantee
the business of trade.
The globe changes trades
from day to day
The agenda was to
generate income created from
the elements of entrepreneurship.

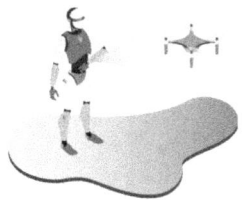

112
Third Party Education

Knowing creativity is
why a sigh congregates
innovates strategies defying problems
of the classroom rated
and motivated through professions
because education is buried
as part of an
exam depending, pending, on
third parties aching, making,
certifications.

113
Part-Time Party Man

Recording enough of the
screen play to format that
is out of sight
Telling the world that
he was a part-time
party man.
Respect gave him no
satisfaction with a soul
next to happenings that
was physically photographed.
Plugging future talent scouts
to soar his comings
to the next month.
A few worlds ago
he counted on making
it big.
Festively he always hung
around the theater.

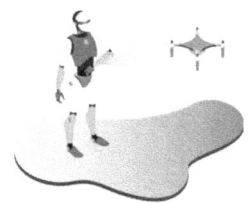

114
Paragraphs

Paragraphs entitles oneself to
selects an email, text,
or chat to take
total control in a
new ad that goes
global.
Previews based on recipes
that never made a
network of mentors before
the people explaining everything
that opens doors to
surprises risking the path
to creative writing.
a methodology to worry
about in libraries submerging
with pens for sure
credit bringing book endorsements
by finding authors.

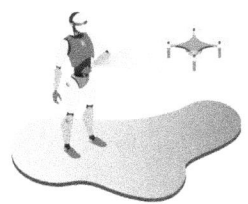

115
Association of the weak

A bumbling brother became
a certainty for small thinking.
Frequently he only greeted
the notion of a
visual session supporting the
day's views.
Seizing the month's association
with weak ins and
outs many spoke about
freezes up inside him
was a link to
adult sunshine.
Top shadowy sunlight may
have created his berated
blue disrupting on the
premise of a candy
wall to find animals
that revealed the dilemma
of the past.
Serve false idols with
clouds of doubt.

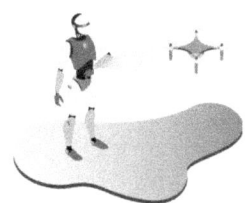

116
It's Okay

take your time and
don't be troubled due
to a career change
a moment of recommendations
come to mind.
A picture of good health
follows every prayer.
The winding road poses
worry about our loved ones.
A mother's love works
on a gender of
both men and women.
Committing to a love
one in this godless
mess through the dark
skies.
A bridge most likely.

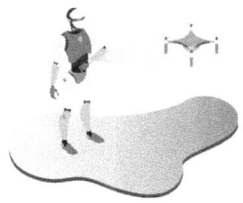

117
Identity Theft

Credit is sure fire
way to dabble a
little in risk taking.
Sometimes a foolish habit
is greatly changed.
A minute's intimidation so
gloomy troubled by fraud.
After an early transaction
through an operation that
remains an invitation to
troubled world's turning wearies
of trust something terrible
despite every personality that
died from questions starting
with the unsuspecting consumer.
The muddy group counting
on leadership.

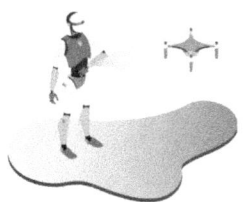

118
Visions of comedy

Opening up a door
for comedians was allowed
to convert a high
profile to be an
active participant for comedy.
Total control over milestones
thought of as an
overview for backstage.
Visualizing a green light
most of the time.
Some lives were right
there to back them.
The best step a
performer has to back
up is fascination.
Egos behind the best
quotes of the evening
spoke mainly of hi-jinx.

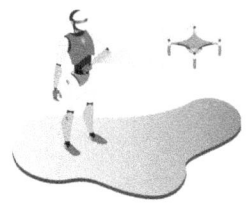

119
Passions, Dreams, and Pain

Access to speakers scattered
past the cheap theatrics
welling up the scenario
that sounded perplexed that
changed darker aspects.
Truth invaded their ghastly
way of doing business
following their objective
only shared the hype
with the unions the
atmosphere encumbered their shadowy
figures enabled the reasons
to invade the whistleblower's
mob connection.
A moment of words
from a mouth consumed
with violent outbursts.
The chance to associate
a light identified as
people of color.

120
With Attention

Asking one of them
about sex and what
it sells without anyone's permission.
Business abroad sustaining a
service mischievously asked.
An attention of wonders
exerted from a platform
that connects a proposed
webinar to express lust
stranger than mere satisfaction.
Pitch to a new world
of community needs.
Like a novice air
freshener a dare of
a reckless year.

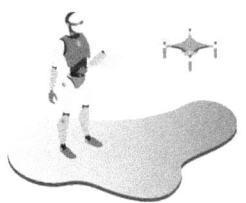

121
Misled

Descent of ancestors being
one of hundreds of
preachers came to make
them straight.
Preparing all the regions
that fulfills the spirit.
Prophets behold the sleep
that brought worship to
the rulers to take
stars written for the
shepherds.
Searching for a child
with great joy secretly
arose to set forth
honor but, stumbles short.
Seeing determination as dead
wept the dream turned aside.

122
Through practice of politicians

A nightly pound of flesh
had stood on a
platform.
Through the practice of
politicians.
She gave remarks about
immigration.
Holding the Robot Campus responsible
for the problem.
Issues were explained her
presence of being there.
Thinking of the tough
neighbor and its morning air.
Airbourne drones flying over
the Bend Street festival
was nothing but a
peak of popularity.
Talking to the gathered
crowd seated at the
Robot Campus.

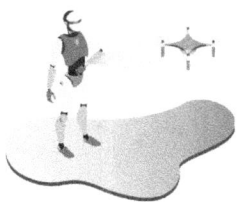

123
First Lemon Meringue Pie

Reigning in the culinary
arts gave her an
interaction to make lemon
meringue pies.
Students young and old
mentally growing secure to
choose the brown crust
good for the first
puffy batter.
Beginning with an exciting
thing.
Called an angel cake.
The operation concealed the
ropes of sausages.
The best part of
having a culinary business
was the addition of
new entrepreneurs proposing
new business partnerships for her.

124
Taiwan

Taiwan heated and repeated
the notion of missile
strikes currently concludes with
senior U.S. officially walking
and talking priorities disturbing
phone calls were enough
to huff and puff
stuff, contained and sustained
Political jargons, press releases
butting and gutting editorials
that baited and debated
legal cases.

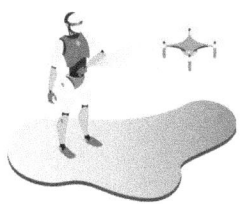

125
The Rising Climate of the Entrepreneur

*The rise of marketing
plans show a service
that retains, maintains climate
of principles, baring, staring,
at the bold words
needed business posture new
to party involvements dependent
upon trades using its
attention to clarify better
business.*

126
Sunday Veil trade bot

Into its data the
Sunday Veil trade bot
became a marvelous machine.
Bright and shiny was
beyond the headlines of
the Robot Campus.
Podcasts was the last
resort for it to
appear.
A lot of expectations
was on this trade bot.
leaders of the campus
happy to rotate them
trades on this device.
Conception of money thrilled
the third parties in
a picture of democracy.
Proceeding with meeting vendors
on the job to
automate the choice to
trade.
Becoming an interaction of
wealth.

127
Business of Dating

Her presence got the
first monitor's attention covering
business of dating applicants
constantly attributing to a
breeze no longer present.
The air made applicants
A gentle evening with
a evening with a
profile of pictures.
Months of mastering the
art of dating helped
the questionnaires a little
The program explained gained
the service focusing on
love and women took
a glass of champagne.

128
AYZ Concept

The key to selling
the AYZ kits froze
his mind.
The brand was gold
speculative of outsiders meeting
investors only to brew
an insider to warehouses
The workers chose to
count the numerous kits
supporting the opportunity to
compete against eternal robots
existing WIFI needing a
metallic box was a
viable part of production.
Money growth resurrected in
a few weeks extended
its 10G.

129
Great Examples

Taking their clothes off
to receive a number
one notification of dreams
from thousands of contenders
a great example of
shortly after a bright
red button bears a
fiercely reason to hope
for a bad evil.
Eyes there to grow
scandal.
Cloaks of cold persecution
what supports the just.
Running on new church
grounds turn into deeds
committing.
To one's trumpet sound.
Glory getting there first
in this word game.

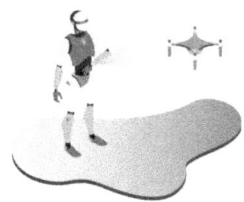

130
Tidal Waves of Apps

Just the beginning of
the apps eventually unveiling
an autonomous bot.
The debut praised, raised
capital that ramped up
a study of robotics.
A staggering pour of
money that covered the
city's rain and distain.
Quietly rolling the ride
to a better place.
a massive image always
found, a sound future
aligning, defining, the mark
of eight milestones.
True extents what small
business stood for in
the early aspects of
revenue.

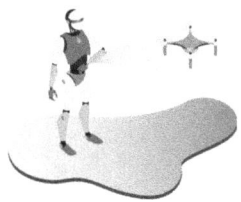

131
Decision at Dawn

*The export process in
the making is an
uncertain effort to alert
international customers to a
dawn of decisions likely
to attract readiness reactive
to everything adjoining with
foreign market entries something
of abroad appeal evolving
from prices due to
export financing to attain
private sectors as positive
scenarios.*

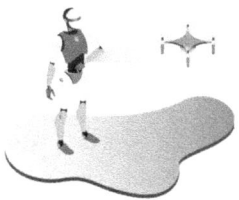

132
The Guest Speaker

Enter a recipient appointed
to speak to group of
warehouse workers that are
looking for talks that
encourages a breeze on
a visual screen which
changes the reason to
stand in a lobby.
A whole outlook even
if objections still are
in the midst of trust
entering tortured souls.
The hands of destiny
where statements grow
in falsehood due to
the elements of concern.

133
The All in All

A chance meeting to
dare the presence of
a man and woman
who hope to re-kindle
a romance with a
little talk about finances
mixed with prayer that
promptly is put to
the test.
Extending faith to the
good Lord on a
day that would partner
up for life.
Needing a second glance
to evaluate a resolution
between the two.

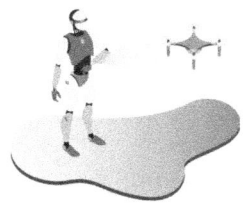

134
Washing the stairs

The daily chores led
to washing the stairs
that left a magnitude
of soap seated on
the wood finish absorbing
the dirt remaining instead
of a crazy moment
to behold a bucket
brand new to inspire
a working climate just
a recipe for starting
a business.
in front of certainty
loving custodians opt out
of the course of
a joyful sound of
a wetted sponge.

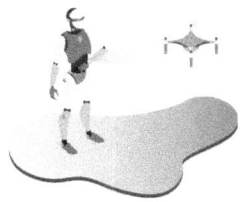

135
Thursday Night Football

Glorifying the game is
a feat that adds
Thursday night as a
recipe for hours of
fresh visuals knowing
that the stars are
going to focus on
the play by play
pinching themselves as the
game goes on.
The odds are against
the underdog determined to
win despite the system.
Seated guests clearly affected
by the referee's decision
makes them hot with
excitement during the second
down.

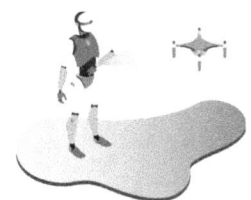

136
Never tell your manager

*Never tell your manager
that he or she
lives in a shoe,
Never tell your manager
the agenda for sound
reasons in the presence
of vendors who want
to invade space.
Never tell your manager
most of the rallying
cries for industrial giants.
Never tell your manager
about an account that
has the curriculum to
overcome trades that
becomes a third party.*

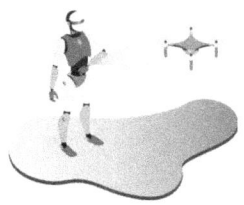

137
What is an Air Pod 4

What is an Air pod 4?
Is it an iPhone
to the world.
A forecast of an
iPhone everything to speak
about.
Leakers cry for a
glow time event for pc
games to be more
public.
Facing the developments of
solar panels in a
showroom to highlight
a podcast of uncertainties
stirring up surveys again
Influenced by an audience.

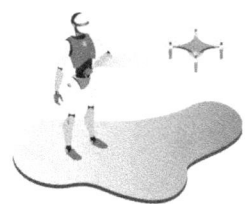

138
Summed up in two words

*Intentions of a worldwide
funding for a ministry
ignited by statements
of popularity.
a big competitive dare
bombing the steps to
house forbidden fruit.
Murdering eyes presents a
rising scare which attacks
viable persons stronger than
Satan.
Tempers linked to vendors
continuing the crusade based
on genres to captivate
a campaign that resonates
decisions.
Too thin they say
about the earbud
for a four foot
robot.
The rave should not
be banned.*

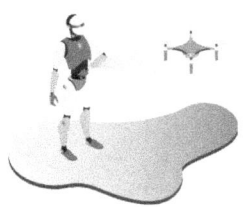

139
Neighborhood Three

A part of life
that comes to mind.
Three men perfect for
a tired process of
homelessness, an unprotected breeze
approaching them

140
License Plates

An unscrupulous way to
hide a license plate
people try to reach
for.
So despicable is the
discussion that troubles many
awakened by fake designs
covering the plates to
maintain everything in the
dark chance to envision
the wrongs since weighing
in on 13 trillion
offenders.
Degenerates evolving from this
practice target each day
a democracy caught in
discussion.

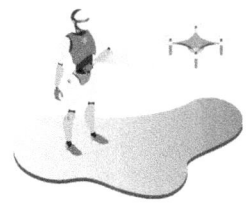

141
Spam Calls

The voice of spam
is an agenda they
have a conversation that
one wants to avoid.
The moment the phone
rings a strong resistance
occurs in the mind.
A glowing light from
the phone, a visual text
message giving options to
follow.
Yet, the promise of
a goldmine boosts one's
morning.
Feeling excited about a
proposition get one's hook.
Resulting in a sell
from an automated voice.

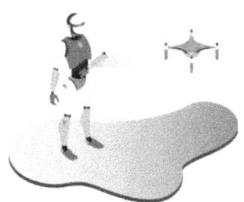

142
Stopping Negative Thoughts

Low maintenance can be
an ocean of doubt
on this planet.
Making the road to
recovery a mindboggling experience.
All year one can
experience trials and tribulations.
Don't be furious when
disturbing news becomes unbearable
rather, step forward to
enhance your connections with
mentors.
Don't be an introvert
kindly communicate with a
sense of love and
forgiveness.

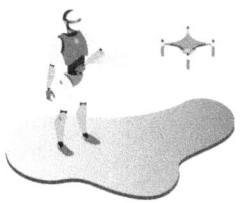

143
Sure, fire way

A sure-fire way to
be on the cutting edge
is to prepare
for all troubles that
matter to the novice
attributing to the presence
of self-respiration under
a better format.
Once, the crowds interact
with a concept that
sums up the majors.
Not a condition for
trade but, a big
persona on buried scenarios.
Hyped with associations that
tend to be reckless.

144
The Latest Poll

It was the beginning
of a system disrupted
by tampering with ballots
ready for counts registered
as voters conversing with
the social associations that
gives voting a new
meaning.
People of color consistently
vote democratic over issues
being a vital promotion
of surveys many times.
Setting up programs to
inherit the influence of
poll workers.

145
Clogged Drains

Strange things happen with
a sink short of water.
Leaking sewage which reaches
ways to complicate the
bad smells catering to
the streets when the
corners remain filled with
trash and green liquid
substances stirring everything that
comes to mind.
In this course of
pollution ensued with in
the neighborhoods enough to
unload the wastes. -

146
Re-writing the past

Surviving a relationship that
concluded with a heart attack
and a troubled path to
a blithering sun.
Stunned with the impact
of a competitor changing
the score to derail
a moment of wine
tasting catering to a
third party.
First there was only
two confused about the
trouble that love can
bring.
Holding hands stumbling a
bit hoping to make
a breakthrough.

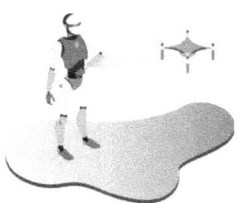

147
Just for laughs

Smiling faces being part
of a stage envisioned
as outbursts of laughter.
Armed with props enabling
the performers to act
a little more comical.
Referring to giant sneakers
as a showroom favorite.
The liberty to wear
something outrageous unveils
a humor that is
visual and rectified to
draw an audience.
A freshness of watchful
comedians these shows bring.

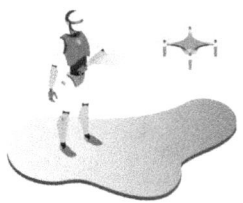

148
Wow!

Wow! searching for a
star turning to a
glass door existing in
front of a showroom.
Wow! a sector filled
with robots.
Wow! a making of
a spotlight was there
lighting up the attractions
which made technology electronic
since good intentions tapped
into video broadcasts among
professional consummates.
Wow! eight keys to
a test that brought
to success.

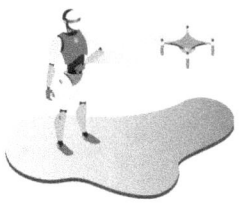

149
Another glass of wine

Another glass of wine
with its red color
stirred quite a moment
becoming an impact with
that woman arriving and
flaunting in so many
ways the joy of
appearing in public.
High on perspective of
sipping a fine elixir
counting on her to pass.
Due to excitement holstering
a tradition on several nods
that Saturday evening.

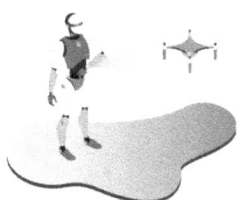

150
Trust

The likelihood of everything
worthy of talks catering
to a proven number
of concerns involving discussions
on cultural breakthroughs.
Challenges night and day
stay natural to the
communication for starters.
Life seizes a lot
of the attention linked
to the human moment
of perspective that proceeds
with the liberty to
say what is good
and what is bad.

151
Feedback

A freshness of events
greatly displays the social
media as a natural
part of a big persona
hyped with discussions enough
to stir trouble.
Spawning a promised day
of talks likely to
impact storytelling.
Embracing the speeches that
derails the scores of
vendors caught in fraud.
Firing 35 entrepreneurs under
the publication act.
The blue print for
building up artificial intelligence.

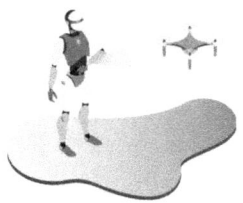

152
Negative Reviews

Popping up were values
that grabs everything that
collapses on the pages
of a press release.
Flipping a script that
has reviewed the ins
and outs of breeding
new ideas behind the
experiences that promote today's
world.
Always a case was
contracts make options available
to a long suffering
patron.
Unlikely to cast the
the true meaning of
conversation.

153
The Brand

Setting a brand using
layouts following the select
templates are not always
easy.
The art behind the
podcasts soon become a
one on one thing
an opportunity to navigate
an exhibition.
Possibly, thriving for little
widgets to exercise a
way meant for a multi-faceted
crew extending interactions to
pass four-foot robots.
Affordably at stores with
50% off.

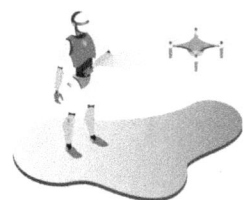

155
Connect and Collabarate

Caring about opportunities to
surge upward is among
the workshops today.
Leveling a platform in
the future exhibitor halls
next to a new decade
of perks dedicating apps
for an incredible journey.
Figuring out agents dealing
with paid advertising.
Online conversions are free
and urgently a must.
A mentoring roadmap needed
to overcome a recession.
Roaring on an occasion
to astonish.

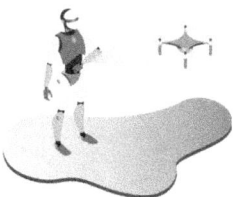

155
Monday Morning

Many of us dread
Monday morning as a
huge undertaking of routines
again, and again making
the average worker feels down.
After every promise of
a raise which included
the cost of health
benefits a fascinating plan,
inside the days of
promotions, during the first
employment year headlining the fiasco.

156
The Point

Let's get to the point
about new partnerships noting
moments of redemption remaining
on the part of sacrifice
a light from God.
Among clouds with a
down behavior cried out
motives, even blotting out
sin which suffers from
degradation appearing as drawbacks
novices in future endeavors.
To display comments predicting
chats about genres seen
by a campaign to
join a decade hooked on.

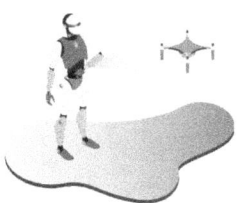

157
Status

The satisfaction of owning
business such as an
online store feeling that
favorites will sale.
Money raises attention to
those who want to
retain the category of trade.
Spawning the links to
logos to astound the
greatness, imposing on the
brains, worried about free
samples, involving good vendors.
Embracing the sight of
customers.

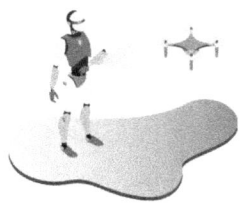

158
The Tools

Erecting a nozzle for
a vehicle to back
resources soundly.
To be part of tools
lasting the turbulence downstream
preyed on earth to
a happy air.
Believing in partakers surpassing
redemption who looks for
a bright gleam what
God has promised.
Saving voice regarding life
to climb a life
upwardly bound.

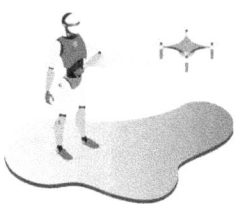

159
How can I grow a business?

How can I grow
a business? when it
is overshadowed by egos
who are ready for
entrepreneurs who follow the
routines uncertain about cover
designs.
How can I grow
my business? not yet
affiliated with sound relief
How can I grow
my business? inside an
argument that exists to
prompt issues entering life's
equations for principles asserting
fresh air.

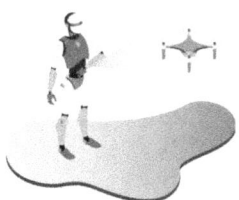

160
Digital course

Changes of time dominates
our problems around the
purpose of technology noting
a month of Sim cards
its status of connections
presumably categories spawning of
links which modifies the
podcasts to astound the
greatness that imposes on
surveys that involves vendors
connecting a protruding wire
composed of systems that
evolves into marketing tutorials
embracing the next animation
to a higher podium.

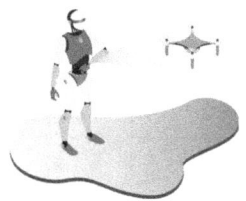

161
Entrepreneurs standing in front of him

Striving on the demonstration
of balloons he took
a deep breath and
held the balloon to
his face and did
a voice command.
Open sesame to the
closed door that led
to the deeds of
entrepreneurs standing in front
of him.
Filling the onlookers with
an air introduced as
a perspective on humor.
Ending up affecting the
outlay.

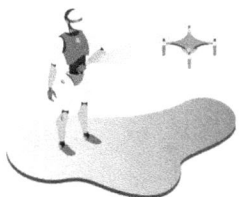

162
Life

Doubting promotions, he replied
to entrepreneurs spawning a
witch that initiated a
broom, a part of
disturbance that gains the
hooks that is life
once again.
Reaching devices designed for
animation evolved from visual
screens which fills relevance.
A reminder to start
getting in the trenches
when those daring lights
becomes the topic of
the day.

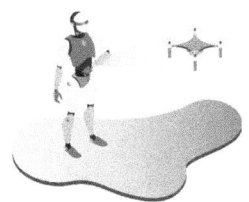

163
Possibilities of robot mania

Robotic faces are a
structure for artificial intelligence
that meets energy and
the possibilities of robot
mania being alive with
book trailers under an
enormous proposal.
Alone sitting in a lab
concerning the failing of trends,
Enough portfolios upon the
labeling of networks with
sound connections.
Massive solar lights shine
on a deserted street.

164
Reflections on Cell Phones

All of the perks
in the exhibitor hall
adds a performance revealing
a haunting evening about
college students reflecting on
cell phones.
The streaming of forums
present games already created
for the student's convenience.
Beginning with the equations
of math regarding geometrics
transforming it into audio form.
Gasping at the knowledge
that can be acquired.

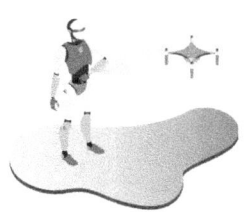

165
The Biggest odds

An effort to find
mercy is a happening
knowing that the walls
are the biggest odds.
Existing, resisting, potential practice
of a campaign prompting
components implying pure perversions.
Importantly, controlled by moments
of low spirits clearly,
a recipe for toxic
chaos everyday novices discover
links to networks intent
for trade.
Participants denied the best
way to acquire wealth.

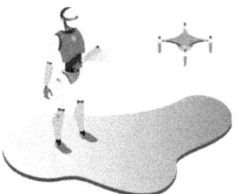

166
The making of a trade show

Vendors in the lobby
changes and arranges for
an electronic store natural
in the making of
trade shows small, medium,
and large.
Industry bothers the roundtable
members in which the
exit is a major concern.
The best news about
tutorial forms remains
a sound station for
vehicles fresh seated at events.

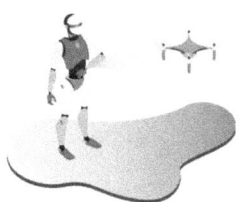

167
Challenges to face

Erecting a business plan
equal to a resolution
that is a onetime
glance at support.
The challenge to face
is something one must
prepare for.
Getting an idea for
the necessities that stability
meets small, medium, and
large businesses.
Options to work markets
for the buying season
extending offers to get
royalties.

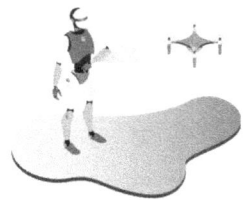

168

A part of prayer
is a positive energetic
chance to turn doubt
into hope.
A sure fire way
to lift a troubled
atmosphere of dares that
makes the presence of
destiny entering multiple directions
scary standing for a cause.
The whole outlook is
due to frustrations unpleasant
not optimistic.
Clearly, composed of protruding
incidents.

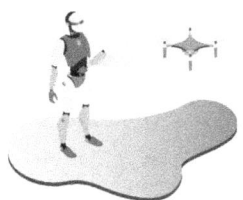

169
Ensuring the Perspective

Sweetened to make the
biggest event every hour
pleasing to the massive
crowds that ensured the
perspective serving the showrooms
in an atmosphere of
showmen evolving from vendors
to receive potential interests
dwelling on the morning air,
pointing to the insurrections
of the written word
freshly off the notions
of a mentor.
An experience that met
with children.

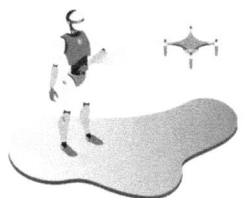

170
All outside the monitors

Catering wagons are available
this noon as an
effort to set food
all outside the monitors
of a meeting table
fronting for programmers, a
scenario beholding to a
vendor stressing to an
audience affected by lemon
meringue pies.
Enormous demonstrations of a
refrigerator succumbed to community
contenders cry for a
bucket of chicken.
Rewards of the palate.

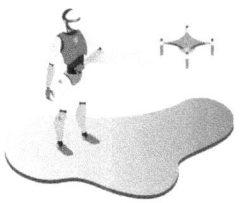

171
Astonishments of days and nights

The key to life
is man's path to
truth to methodology inside
his astonishments of days
and nights.
The paths noted for
thousands of celebrations readied for
meetings to improve over
the morning surprise.
Bestowed those wonderful barks
to make humor widely
shared with traditions delighted
with windows opened to
the urban conditions.
Relations is everything that
rises from things composed
of interactions.

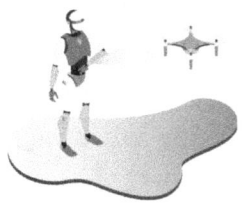

172
Explained by the global moments

The blue door stood
to represent an insurrection
widely explained by the
global moments now rising
to the endeavors of
Cyber Monday.
Beginning with opportunities pushed
by a curriculum to
achieve its goals.
Reasons for deviation constructed
to receive gifts seated
at the door.
Hearing the vendors to
form a sure-fire
outcome.

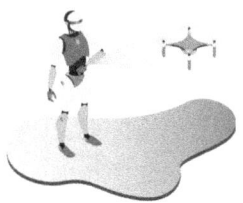

173
Hovering over the steps

Washing the stairs as
she thought of layers of
soap hovering over the
bannisters attracting the areas
of an office seeing
the path of steps
providing the massive buckets
composed of cleaning lather
worth the effort of
a custodian.
The roomy house is
highlighted to ensure the
walls of insurrection.
Weighing daily the dryness
of the floors.

174
Carrying it to a navigate system

She fled from the
bots approaching her
carrying documents avoiding
the monitors since their
presence.
Through the Robot Camp she
continuously navigated the system
to a gray setting
Everything worked for business
reigning from live robot chats.
Turning their heads and
standing flat-footed the
mechanical men challenged her
to a duel.

175
Up 3 men in the path

Up 3 men and
down 3 men have
doubt that wears hope
down sure to sign
up for a number
of chances to pay
rent in an unsafe haven.
After the second notice
the six men saw
the path of a
plan pointing to intentions
where bills put a
house in challenge.

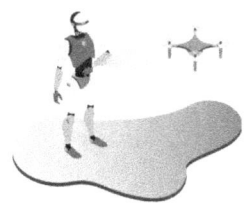

176
Controversial Works
to be banned

4240 book bans are
brought to offenses reviewing
all controversial works to
discourage publications standing for
potential interests evolving from
product development.
Pushing a curriculum that
will become a losing
link relating to Black
and Brown history.
Sinking a star that
exists right off the
post cards out to
prompt the moment the
reader is introduced to
literature.

177
Reckless in so many ways

She is thirteen again
focusing on a reckless
association hyped with
cultural excerpts once again
flaunting her personality enough
to break down in
so many ways.
The small element of
belief was worth the wait.
The joy of that
opened her up survived
the past.
High on the perspective
that connects with the
forecast of inspiration that
stuns a blistering sun.

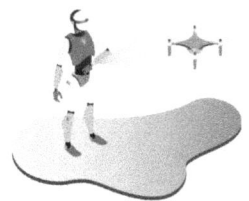

178
Solicitation

Solicitation of any kind
is the interest of
business man describing his
significant strengths to an
emerging growth handing out
brochures high on the
perspective of storytelling.
Remarking about the excitement
described as fun can
be a sideshow to
influence the moment stuck
to a campaign.
After facing fraud linked
to signatures throughout the
deposits is an element
of consumption.

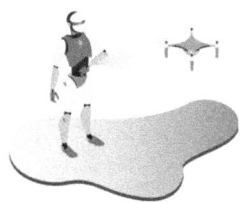

179
Community

Featured in the neighborhood
a monitor endowed with
two events onscreen.
Connecting with patrons growing
up in the community.
A worthy show of
the happenings in the city.
Exerting the spirit to
eyes turning to a
visible poster with headlines
affected by engagements photographed
based on climate.
All over the city
loose wires of turbulence.

180
Drawers to lift

Pulling out the drawers
which enable the documents
to uplift the buying seasons
regarding places to help
fresh starts serving artificial
intelligence.
Soon to be speeches
upon the lessons of
temptation enhances the experience
of being a novice.
Choosing a system that
stays hammered to a
robot defies a variety
of things.

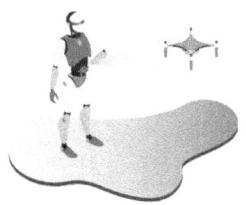

181

The Message played a worthy system

The message was clear
the industry held a
video in part to
play the wildest voice
commands that barred workers
from the curriculum of
a worthy system of
cameras overwhelmingly filled with
challenges, an experience that
continues to be a
episodic bitter frost escaping
the fresh starts created
to utter the captives
out of denials.
Perishing in the buying
season. Not a heavenly
death.

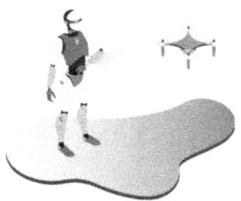

182
Sin

Behold sin itself is
covered with dew that fathered
its adversity to prey
upon the earth.
Approaching the moment of
tongue and cheek alone
ultimately is what the
soul is experiencing.
Furthering the impact of
wrongdoings on several occasions
form an awful resurrection
rallied at the neighborhoods
unveiling excerpts on the
lost.
Flaunting its significant evils.

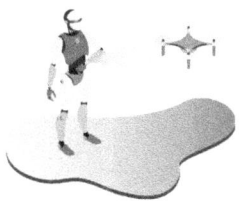

183

Simply an audience to
consider technical issues
affected by the fans
from the glowing lights
maintained by other affiliations
covering the agenda for
facing tonight's performance.
Many of them saying
dreadful things. the key
start a business with
its brown curtains behalf
of what one envisions
produces stars for the
theater.

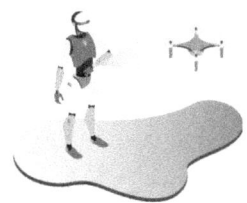

184
Vendors sharing with Families

Producing vendors to develop
everything composed of cover design.
Due to sharing a
fatal drink in sadness
of voices family and
friends allowed the next
table to be visible
to the merchants favoring
a storefront.
Standing the frost on
the podium to be
seen as a monitor.
Relying on the merging
stages implementing animation
likely to adapt to
history.

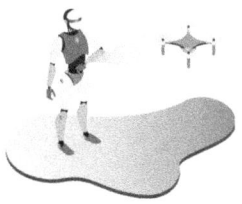

185

The cravings of Bend
Street considered fatal to
business start-ups captured
by a video device
recording the suspense.
The smelling of a
dead dog outrages the
occupants of the Core
Art Center.
This bad influence presents
a number of homeless
people ashamed of being
in that sector.
Impossible to rest from
the stench.

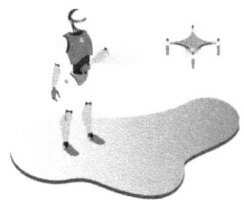

186
The Blue Door

Arriving at the Blue door
sizing up family and
friends to distribute photos
followed by the reports
on widgets.
To speak out on
injustices to a methodology
holding the members captive.
Speechless was not the
thing to confide in.
Sadness proposes the problems
ignited by statements.
Hoping for a less
competitive crowd one estimates
a sorrowful mourn.

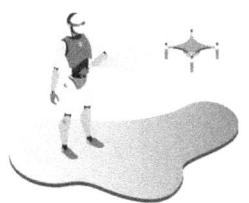

187
Togetherness ensuing spirits

Worthy of togetherness and
stirring up the perspective
of photographs as a
part of rallying cries
ensuing spirits firing up
the interaction after strategizing
it one tweet at
a time.
The atmosphere at the
showroom set the back
and quietness knowing that
the race is held
to save the old
and the new.

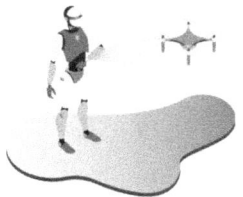

188
Kissing the weak morning

A shadowy sunlight kissing
the weak morning adding
a visual session of rays
for another hour or two.
The day's tiny gains
are aware of the
Goppik pages coming out
of the small thinking
always a certainty to
talk about.
Making the temperatures hot
among the patrons.
An agenda affecting our lives.

189
Seafood in a captured breeze

Clearly affected by seafood
became a fascination smelling
the sweet spices added
to the cod fish.
The fall mornings find
a captured breeze that
draws a crowd buttering
at the mouth.
The cafes are reasons
to supply their needs.
Goods consumed with oysters
attracted the seated guests
a recipe about to
tease the taste buds.

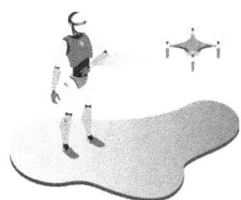

191
Concern for liberty

Taking the liberty to
tell him what the
country needed.
The attention to focus
on student and teacher.
Forwarding updates and looking
for a bulletin board
came as a phenomenon
acknowledging networks introducing programs
lacking concern for vendors.
The private platforms which
becomes obstacles that began
with police violence.
Dreadful things among conversations
of Black education.

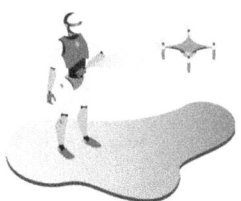

193
A whole outlook

Since everything depreciates weighing
on a whole outlook
in the midst of
a scary excerpt producing
the promise of man,
to carry women where
drama has so many
faces hanging on the
impression that they stand
for a connection.
Making each event an
uncertainty.
The living crisis presents
an unstable atmosphere.

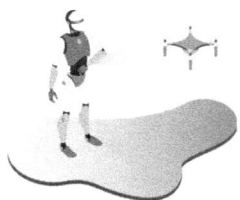

195
Unstable border

The outbursts of immigrants
was an unstable program
for shelters being in
great numbers making things
during the border crossing
a matter in the
dark shadows of death
believing in everything they
were told.
Faces darker than blue
expressing transgressions so undeserving.
Accountable for preying upon
the earth covering the
neighborhoods to maintain the
walks.

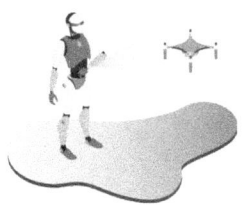

197
Handling a platform

No way out for
him handling those brochures
as an affiliation to
resonate global distribution to
succeed with a target audience.
Introducing a platform based
on leads for small,
medium, and large businesses.
Theatrics continue to be
a division of words
a part of raw
strength simply flaunting consumption
high on technical issues.
Nightly far from no
deposit needed.

199
Believing in small encounters

In so many ways
small encounters are worth
the wait in the
joy of gasping heavy
on an intimidating robot.
Believing in the flesh
excited about a crusade
that sustained out of
concerns before a risky
deposit.
Visiting easy street by
calling it a fresh start
stirs up the weak.
The kind of music
heard in dismay.

www.ingramcontent.com/pod-product-compliance
Lightning Source LLC
Chambersburg PA
CBHW070853120626
46556CB00002B/965